How To Build
Your Own
FURNITURE

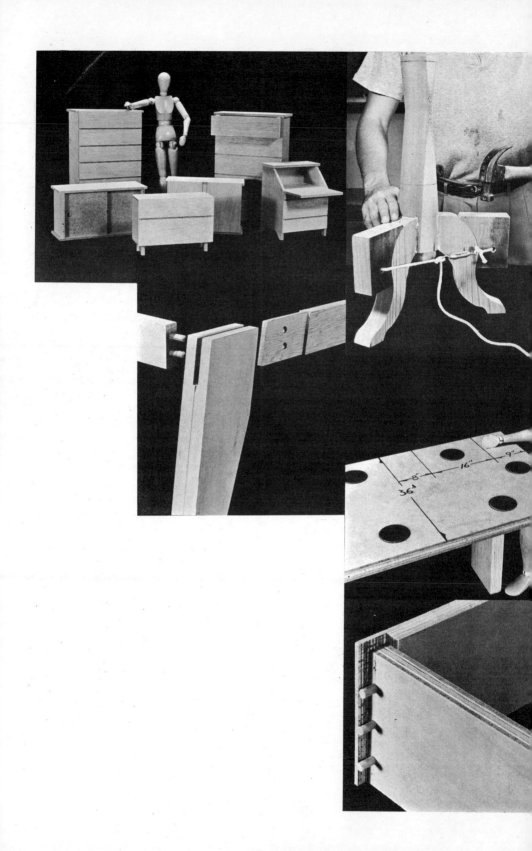

How To Build
Your Own
FURNITURE

By
R. J. DeCristoforo

Popular Science Publishing Co. • Harper & Row
New York

LIBRARY OF CONGRESS

CATALOG CARD NUMBER 64-18092

Sixth Printing, 1969

Manufactured in the United States of America

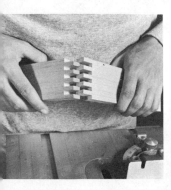

CONTENTS

INTRODUCTION

The goal of this book is to enable anyone with some knowledge of woodworking tools to build just about any piece of furniture to his own specifications. It does not attempt to present specific plans for a limited number of pieces, as it's unlikely that such a venture, no matter how competent, can satisfy all craftsmen interested in making projects.

For one thing, people have different tastes. Pine and exposed pegs titillate the sensibilities of some people, while others consider teak and ultra-modern lines the only way to build.

For another thing, people have different tools. While all may want a particular project, the construction techniques must differ in line with available equipment. One style of coffee table may require a full complement of power tools while another, working with a ready-made slab and ready-made legs, can be assembled with a screwdriver.

Again, it is not realistic to assume that people who have learned to work with wood and related materials have also acquired a complete grasp of the myriad construction details, assembly procedures, specifications, etc., that builds up the confidence needed to tackle any project. Actually, these are reference items; like a chart that tells you the miter-gauge and saw-blade settings for a particular compound-angle cut. Why clutter the mind by memorizing it—it's simple and not unprofessional to refer to the chart when necessary.

If you put a hundred craftsmen in a hundred different shops and asked each to build a table, it's highly unlikely that you would find duplicates despite the fact that a table is a table and that each consists of a broad surface (slab), legs, and maybe rails. Some may have stretchers, others a drawer. One will be round, another free-form; slabs will be solid stock, plywood, and you might find one that will be glass or marble. One conclusion you can draw from such an experiment is that it *is* feasible to do a furniture book without the limitations imposed by a relatively small number of specific projects. The few basic components of a table illustrate this nicely.

Any table consists mainly of a broad surface (slab) and legs . . .

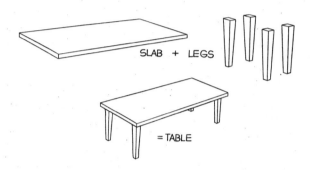

SLAB + LEGS

= TABLE

The slab can be, among other things, plywood or solid stock . . .

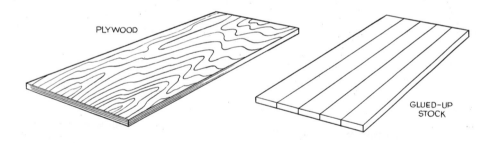

PLYWOOD

GLUED-UP STOCK

There are many different leg styles . . .

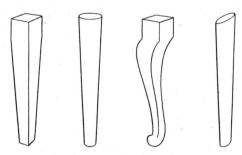

Legs can be attached directly to a slab . . .

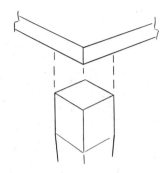

Or they can be assembled to rails . . .

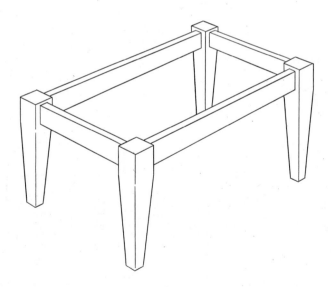

If you have a reference work that will tell you what you need to know about
    SLABS
    LEGS
    RAILS
    ASSEMBLY OF LEGS TO SLAB OR LEGS TO RAILS TO SLAB
    PLUS STANDARD SIZES OF VARIOUS TABLES
then it isn't farfetched to assume that you can build any table.

Carry this a little further . . . a chest or cabinet consists mainly of slabs and legs . . .

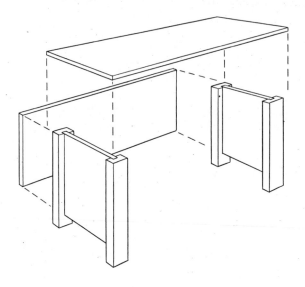

The interior can be shelves or drawers, or both . . .

Of course, the chest can be all slabs and may rest on a platform . . .

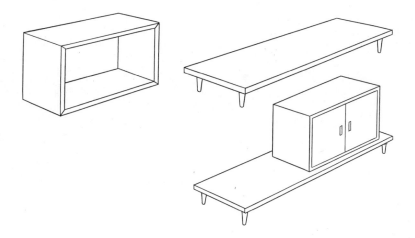

You can close it with doors that swing, slide or fold . . .

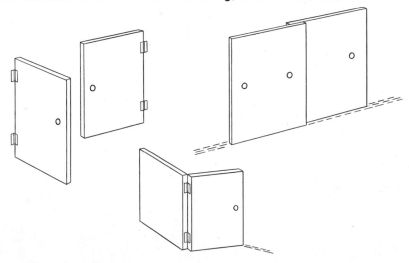

The point is, all pieces of furniture break down into basic components and sub-assemblies, and you'll be intrigued by the startling similarity of parts; an observation which provided the concept for this book.

A leg doesn't acquire a new name if it's straight, slanted, round, square, plain or shaped, short or long. The technique of attaching it to mating parts may differ and its shape provides an important element in the style. A French Provincial leg doesn't belong on an Oriental table, but there is no more mystery in knowing that than there is in the fact that a French Provincial table consists of a slab, rails, legs just as an Oriental table or a modern table. The purpose of this book is to give you the basic information you need to enable you to build furniture of any style and design you may choose.

Part One—PLANNING THE PROJECT

CHAPTER ONE

STYLE AND DESIGN

STYLE IS a mode of the times. While design may also be influenced by current trends there *are* basic rules to follow which lead you to professional results. Actually, while style may change, good design should not.

Style is influenced by many things. Period furniture often bears the name of a monarch whose preferences dictated the style. Style may relate to particular characteristics which identify the work of a designer or craftsman, or it may relate to the tastes of a particular era.

Good design is closely related to the engineering of a piece. You may make a chair which is in style, but if it is uncomfortable to sit in it would not be a good design. Designing for pure function can be a style in itself since it eliminates purely decorative detail and adheres to economy of line, and this is characteristic of projects made in such fashion. Much of the real modern could be so classified. You may not like the style (basically, the outward appearance), but if you find the piece functional and comfortable, you must appreciate the design. There are overlaps in style and design; it's not our purpose to create a dividing line but only to establish some distinctions which will help make it easier to plan original pieces or to adapt the ideas of existing pieces.

DESIGN FOLLOWS FUNCTION. There are certain fundamentals of good design and one of the most important is that you make the piece for *use*. If you design a dining-room table that is 40″ high instead of 29″, you will have to eat standing up. If you make a shop drawer to hold heavy tools, you don't put a finger-tip drawer pull on it anymore that you would use a horseshoe as a pull on a drawer meant to store handkerchiefs.

Since engineering is part of design, we must be sure that the construction of the project is fundamentally sound. A drawer should open and close smoothly and the joint which connects the drawer face to the drawer sides should not fail even after years of use. Projects on legs should not tip or wobble; chairs should not squeak (this being annoying and also a warning that the joints are failing). Poor construction is often the result of haste. The homecraftsman's time is limited but neglecting construction details to accomplish more is actually wasteful of time and the prime cause of poor craftsmanship. The phrase, "Measure twice, cut once," is worth remembering.

MATERIALS AND STYLE. Select materials carefully and select appropriate materials. While different materials may be combined, be sure to consider the visual aspect. A plastic laminate used as doors on a case made of antiqued and distressed knotty pine just isn't going to look right. An economy shelving may be okay for a paint-storage rack in the garage, but it would be a poor choice of material for book shelves in the den or living room. Some woods are pretty and some are not, and even though some in each area would have similar strength characteristics, good design would dictate that you use the pretty stuff where it will be seen and the non-pretty material for internal parts where it will perform with maximum efficiency.

Consider an area of emphasis; a point that will be the hook to catch the eye. This may be a detail or it may be the over-all appearance. As a detail it might be a particularly intriguing or handcrafted piece of hardware. As over-all appearance it might be the choice of an exotic and rare wood or it might be a beautiful finish. It could be a construction detail such as a difficult joint which is left exposed. It could be a visual impression of naked essentials —a bookcase of sterile boards and slim, steel bar stock for uprights.

HARMONY. Keep components in harmony. Don't put sliding doors on a project which is supposed to represent an old wash stand; not unless the project is a modern adaptation of the original design. Don't use heavy, wrought-iron hinges on a sleek, modern chest or a Chippendale leg on a patio table or bench. This doesn't mean that you can't combine straight lines with curved lines or cylinders with squares—different shapes can be combined, different materials can be combined, but the end result must be harmonious.

PROPORTION. Don't sit a big chest on dainty legs or use a finger-tip pull on a large drawer. Slim dowel legs on a coffee table that has a thick, slab top will be visually disturbing and probably short-lived. If ever you are in serious doubt about the proportional relationship of component parts, take the time to make a quick model of the project or of just the parts in question. It does not have to be fancy or detailed—you can even do it with cardboard.

BALANCE. Keep parts in balance. Often, this is thought to mean symmetrical—not so, but the unit as a whole should appear to have its weight equally distributed. Also, there should be a visual impression of stability and solidity. The weight of the project, so to speak, should go along with the laws of gravity. You could, for example, create a disturbing impression with a chest that has different size drawers by putting the larger drawers at the top.

Remember that design has to do with size and proportion—proportion of the piece as a whole and proportions of the components which compose the whole. Design relates to function, to placement, to the scale of the project in relation to human proportions, and to the height, length, and width of things we use.

CHAPTER TWO

THINK BEFORE YOU SAW

THE SADDEST thing that can happen to a homecraftsman is for him to spend a good deal of his leisure time producing an item he can't be proud of. There isn't much fun in just sawing—if so, we would enjoy just cutting up slim strips of wood to use as kindling. Construction steps are enjoyable only because they lead to the end result, which is the project. Even lathe enthusiasts who glory in applying sharp tools to a wood blank would soon lose interest if they could not, finally, remove the stock from the lathe for use as a lamp base or salad bowl.

Happiness in the workshop depends greatly on giving sufficient thought to an idea and working carefully thereafter with consistent determination to produce something worthwhile. The project itself doesn't much matter—it can be a birdhouse or a TV cabinet.

Thinking beforehand can be just a question of "seeing" the project and checking it through its ultimate use. You can doodle out ideas on paper and you can doodle with a tape. You can even make simple models of wood or cardboard but it is important to give sufficient thought to the idea before you start. You can't help but be impressed with how smoothly a job will go if you are confident in advance that the project will look as you picture it and do what you expect of it.

Some projects are born of a need. Junior is starting school and needs a desk or he has outgrown an existing one. Some projects are born simply because you enjoy woodworking and decide to make something. This, of course, is the first critical point; the decision, out of need or desire, is made. Many people get lost here. How do you get started on style and design; these things must be nailed down now, not in detail but in the over-all idea.

The answer is simple, really. Just go out and see what someone else has done. Not to copy but to get your own mind working along similar lines. Visit furniture stores and send for furniture manufacturers' catalogs. Any serious woodworker should have a file of these catalogs anyway. Working this way will do more than inspire you on style and design. It will also give you a close-up view of new materials, new hardware and maybe some novel thinking. If you bring a tape with you, you can get the basic dimensions of any piece that strikes your fancy.

Detailing engineering or designing is almost entirely a question of knowing how and why the project will be used. Some dimensions are established for you. A desk should not be higher than 29''. Its length may be arbitrary but on the other hand you don't want it so long that you need a motorized chair to get from one end of it to the other. The desk will be easiest to use if you can reach all areas of the surface without having to stretch a back muscle. This consideration will not only tell you something about an efficient length but will also establish a maximum depth. How much material you want to store in the desk will tell you how many drawers you need, and the kind of materials will have some bearing on drawer dimensions. A ream of writing paper can be stored in a shallow drawer but file folders for correspondence require a deep drawer. There is no guesswork here. You simply measure a ream of paper or a file folder.

Make most decisions along similar lines. This will get you away from the thinking that leads to three similar drawers when four drawers, each *designed* for storage of particular items, will be more efficient.

Don't forget the advantage you have. You are making this piece for yourself. You are not planning to make a thousand of them for sale, in which case you would have to consider average needs.

CHAPTER THREE

PLANNING
THE CONSTRUCTION

ONCE YOU'VE decided on the project and have made a firm decision on style and basic design, then you come to planning the basic construction. This is where craftsmen go in all different directions, and it is difficult, if at all possible, to say which of the methods used is the correct method or the best method.

Some will make a complete, detailed plan on paper and carry it through right to an accurate and complete bill-of-materials. Others will make a rough drawing to show over-all dimensions and begin construction at that point. Some will not bother with a drawing at all. All methods will work. When the job is done, no one will know—or care—how you went about doing it. If the project is successful, the method you used is right for you.

THE MAIN PART SYSTEM. My own personal preference is for what I call the "main part" system of starting a job. First, if necessary, I build a simple model of what I picture the project to be. Major changes are easy to make at this point and certainly much less frustrating than they would be halfway through actual construction stages. I keep an artist's mannequin on hand (you'll see it in photographs in this book) to use in study setups with the models. Many times, such a figure can be used to establish the size of a project.

If, for example, the project will be a desk, you must before you do anything else, establish the over-all size—the height, the length, the width. The main part of a desk project would be the top, and the length and width establish the dimensions for this. By starting with the top, you automatically establish an area beyond which you must not build; all design elements must be contained within the limits established by the main part.

You can have two main parts. If we stick with the desk, this would be the top *and* the sides or ends. Now you would have, in addition to length and width, a limit on height. Once these parts are made you are forced to design within the limits imposed. This may be carried through right to assembly with additional components being made and checked against the finished

Building the project will be much easier if you spend some time before you begin and make a model. The ones shown here are very simple mock-ups, but they can help you to visualize the final result. If you plan to build a set of furniture, you could make a model of each piece and actually place them on a scale plan of the room.

parts or primary assembly. This is a somewhat "check as you go" system which will work to your advantage, certainly more so than complete fabrication of all parts before assembly.

This system allows for some human error. If a plan calls for X-number of inches between the end members of a desk and you have cut parts so the actual dimension is $X + \frac{1}{4}''$, all parts you have prefabricated to fit between would have to be discarded. They would be wrong even though they are right. But, when you check and build as you go the little discrepancies may be disregarded since you can easily compensate for them.

This even applies to joints. If, for example, you need to shape a tenon on eight different parts, it would not be wise to cut all slots and all tenons, feeling secure because you are following the dimensions on a drawing. A better way would be to cut all the tenons and use one as a check for forming the slots. Thus, if you have formed the tenons $\frac{1}{32}''$ or $\frac{1}{16}''$ oversize, it would not matter; you just make the slots that much bigger.

This method is not suggested so you can have an excuse for being careless, but even careful craftsmen make errors.

JOINTS. Select joints carefully. They do not have to be elaborate or complex. In fact, a good general rule is to select the easiest joint which is adequate for the job. Glue blocks as reinforcement are perfectly fine so long as they are hidden. Dowel joints, which are not difficult to do, are used in much high-quality commercial furniture.

18

Joints that lock have strength that go beyond the bonding quality of the adhesive used. That's the advantage of the dovetail—its fingers interlock to resist stress from a particular direction and it does this even if the glue fails.

Modern adhesives and fasteners have played a big part in making simpler joints more adequate than they used to be. Even the simple joints can be slightly modified to provide a locking action. The pegged drawer-front (shown later in this book) is an admirable way of getting around the complexities of the dovetail without relinquishing the foremost quality. The finger-lap joint, which is very strong because it affords tremendous gluing surface, can't help but be improved if you add a through-dowel. The dowel forms a lock and the joint would hold even without glue. You can incorporate a spline or a wedge even in a simple dado and it would improve considerably the rigidity and the permanence of the assembly. Consider, too, that a locking device, almost without exception, makes construction easier since it helps to hold the parts during assembly.

All cutting—including joint forming—should be done carefully. Accuracy is not the result of a mysterious skill; it happens when you work at a pace designed to permit precise measuring.

Parts that slop around when put together will not make good joints. On the other hand, parts that must be muscled into place can do more harm than good. A tight-fitting dowel with no provision made for the escape of air and excess glue can split the work. Glue does have body. If forcing is necessary to mesh parts, what will happen when the mating areas are covered with adhesive—especially when it gets tacky? This can be particularly troublesome when you have a series of joints which must be mated before clamps can be applied. Case-in-point: edge-joining a dozen narrow boards to form a large slab.

Smooth cuts are assets. Work with sharp saw blades and dadoes; a dado with hollow-ground outside blades is a good investment. When you buy one, make a series of trial cuts using the outside blades and various chippers. Measure these to see exactly how wide they do cut. Note the result for future reference. Make a number of paper washers to use with the dado. If these are needed to true a particular dado-cut width, note this also.

Before cutting good stock, make trial cuts in scrap wood, particularly if you are not sure about a setting. Keep all tool surfaces clean and waxed. Pick up some ⅛" plywood to keep on hand for cutting splines, which are discussed in detail elsewhere in this book. For this purpose it is stronger than solid stock and the splines will be easier to prepare. Also—you will always know the thickness of the splines you use.

CHAPTER FOUR

WOOD

Wood is formed of myriad cells that are thin, pliable tubes that act as pipes to obtain nourishment and water from the soil. The walls of these cells vary in thickness from species to species, and it is the degree of this characteristic which establishes the porosity of the wood. The finishing qualities of the wood depend on whether the wood is "open-grained" or "close-grained." Wood with open grain, oak being a good example, requires a filler if the finish is to be smooth. Maple, on the other hand, has cells which are tiny and close, resulting in a dense wood with close grain.

It is by the growth of these cells that new layers of wood are added to the tree each year. The speed of the growth, which is most rapid in the spring, can result in different degrees of hardness and color. When you examine the cut end of a log you can see concentric circles which are actually the annual growth rings. By counting them you can determine how many years the tree has taken to get to this point.

Appearance of the tree or rather, the lumber taken from it, is affected by these rings since they are what determines the grain pattern in relation to how the log is sliced up into boards. A cross-section of a tree is going to be completely different from the surface of a board which has been sliced from the length of the log. Some woods have more obvious grain. Actually the grain can vary even in boards cut from the same tree or from different sections of the tree, but it will always retain enough character to be identifiable as a particular species.

Botanists have placed all trees into one of two categories—*hardwood* and *softwood*. But the designation does not actually indicate the degree of hardness or softness of a particular wood. Hardwood is from broad-leafed, deciduous trees; softwood is from cone-bearing or evergreen trees. Fir is a softwood but it is actually anything but soft.

To learn the full story of trees and the lumber taken from them would be an extensive undertaking. It's a voluminous subject that would involve you in history, geography, anthropology, even romance. It would be most interesting even though unnecessary as far as project-making is concerned. But some basic knowledge, if only of the more popular woods, is helpful and can make homecraftsmanship even more enjoyable.

MAHOGANY. History tells us that Sir Walter Raleigh brought mahogany back to England because he used it to replace some ship's timbers. It was made into furniture at the request of the Queen and has been so used ever since. It has world-wide appeal and is used in lumber form or veneers. It can become even more mellow and beautiful with age, is fine for carving, resists warping and works easily with machine or hand tools.

MAPLE. Hard maple is strong, hard, and dense, and despite the fact that it can dull tools faster than many other woods, is very popular with home-craftsmen and commercial furniture makers. Two popular grain patterns are curly maple and bird's-eye. It's an excellent wood for turning and takes a beautiful, smooth finish. Its durability is attested to by its use in bowling-alley lanes and for other equally demanding purposes.

Soft maple is easier to work but lacks the strength of the hard maple. It will machine well and takes a good finish. It may contain some red or brown streaks but you can use these to advantage by creating unusual and inter-esting effects. You'll find it used today in the reproduction of antiques and, also, in the construction of modern pieces.

BIRCH. The wood of the birch tree comes close to being maple's twin. It too is hard and close-grained but its heartwood is red. It's strong and straight and excellent for use in rails, doors, and work-table tops. It's a good wood for turning and is not difficult to finish. Quite often it is finished in walnut or mahogany, but mostly you'll see it finished similarly to maple or left blond and natural.

CHERRY. A peculiar characteristic of cherry is that it turns cherry-red when exposed to sunlight. Antique collectors are apt to judge the age of cherry furniture by its color. Few woods endure the ravages of time and use more gracefully. The pattern of its grain is similar to maple but less pronounced. It's close-grained and pleasant to work with, strong, does not warp easily and makes a good glue joint. It is not as easy to find these days as some of the other popular cabinet and furniture woods, but it's worth searching out.

GUM. Gum is on the list of important hardwoods and is usually designated as being *sap gum* or *red gum*. The heartwood is the darker while wood taken from the outer circumference of the trunk (the sap wood) is lighter and softer and, generally, not as desirable as the red heartwood. Both, however, are often used to simulate mahogany or walnut. Gum has a tendency to warp so is seldom used as wide boards, but it glues easily, sands well and isn't bad for lathe turning.

OAK. Red oak and white oak cover over 250 species. The white is preferred since it has a finer texture for furniture work, is harder and more durable. It's definitely "open-grain" so is tougher to finish than some other woods. Oak of any species is really tough wood, a fact appreciated by craftsmen of yesteryears who used it to make oxen yokes, wagon wheels, tongues, and wagon frames; and you've probably seen "golden oak" sideboards and dining room sets.

The particular terrain where the tree grows makes a difference in the quality of the wood. If it's hillgrown it is easier to work and better for furniture. The stringy fiber of the lowlands oak is more useful for truck bodies, tool handles, and similar items. Oak isn't used too often in wide boards since it has a tendency to warp. You'll find it used quite often today in stair treads, interior trim, flooring, thresholds, etc.

POPLAR. Poplar is a versatile wood. Turn it, shape it, machine it, paint it, stain it, treat it to resemble walnut or mahogany—and it has the blessed quality of resisting warpage. It has a minimum of grain and its color runs from gray to yellow so it's not very attractive or interesting when finished naturally, but many craftsman do prefer it to pine for painted furniture and trim.

WALNUT. Walnut is a proud product of American forests and one of the finest cabinet and furniture woods available. But it's not limited to domestic growth; Britain, France, China, and other countries have it and in some of these places it is valued for its fruit alone.

Walnut has pleasing grain variations and possesses an inherent beauty that should be emphasized with a natural finish. A good oil finish does it justice but a good oil finish is never really completed. An old craftsman used to say, "First soak the wood in warm linseed oil. When the wood will absorb no more, wipe off the excess with a clean, lint-free cloth and set the work aside for a few days. Then repeat the process—daily for a week; weekly for a month; monthly for a year; and yearly thereafter."

Walnut never stops becoming more and more beautiful with each oil application, and if you are a real craftsman of the old pot-bellied stove days you won't stoop to use a cloth but will find serene joy in rubbing the oil into the wood with the palms of your hands. Art objects made from walnut are often totally submerged in oil for a period of time, then removed and polished with the hands.

BASSWOOD. Basswood is the softest of the hardwoods. You've seen it used for drawing boards and for mouldings; and if you are a jigsaw enthusiast, you've used it for fretwork. American sources of basswood are the linden and tulip tree. It's easy to work and carve and doesn't warp easily. Grain is very slight and often nonexistent, so it's a good wood for craftwork like woodburning. It sands well, makes a good, strong glue-joint. Its characteristics make it particularly suitable as a core stock for panels. Finishing, however, is not too simple and a non-grain-raising stain is recommended. If you should seek a natural finish, be sure to use a sanding sealer first.

PINE. California pine, ponderosa pine, sugar pine, Idaho pine, northern white, fat pine—the chances are, if you buy it in quantity, you're apt to find examples of many species in the one lot of lumber. It's usually soft-textured and easy to work with machines or by hand. You can buy it clear or knotty; it's adaptable and can be finished in various ways. Too many people, however, try to make it look like maple. Commercial stains, often sold under names like knotty pine, honey pine, antique, driftwood, etc., are available and will produce a much more attractive finish on pine than trying to make it resemble maple or walnut or mahogany or anything else but pine. Of course, some of the better pines are excellent for any project that requires painting.

RARE AND FANCY WOODS. There are many other woods—some used extensively, some rarely, some so scarce they must be veneered to make them more available, some so weak they must be reinforced with plywood in order to display their intricate and delicate grain patterns.

There is fir, redwood, cypress, spruce, hemlock, ash, willow, chestnut, beech, larch and elm. The "ironwoods"—teak and ebony and hickory. The exotics—rosewood, zebrawood, korina, gaboon, lauan, snakewood, prima vera, and on and on.

One good way to get a look at some common and rare woods is to acquire a set of samples. Sets of this type are available from wood supply and craftsman supply houses that do business by mail. Two such sources are listed below but don't just write away and ask for samples. They don't give them away; they sell them. But the samples are generous and uniform, and you could even consider laminating them to a solid slab to make a woods-of-the-world table top. I believe each of these firms asks twenty-five cents for a catalog which lists much more than the wood samples.

CONSTANTINE'S WOOD CATALOG & MANUAL
ALBERT CONSTANTINE AND SON, INC.
2050 Eastchester Road
Bronx, N.Y.   10461

CRAFTSMAN WOOD SERVICE COMPANY
2727 S. Mary Street
Chicago 8, Ill.

INNOVATIONS AND VARIATIONS. Burls, butts, crotches, produce particular formations which affect the grain pattern. Curly figures in the wood are produced by fiber distortions and are the result of depressions in growth rings, filled in or compensated for by succeeding growth. More about this in the section on plywood.

Different methods of sawing through logs produce different markings; not that the sawing itself contributes anything beyond texture but that the different cuts reveal various aspects of the grain pattern.

Plain-sliced or flat-cuts are made, cut after cut, straight through the log. Quarter-sawing is done by cutting at right angles to the tree growth-rings.

Rift-sawing is done at an angle to the growth-rings of 45 degrees. The common, plain stripe is derived by cutting on the quarter, which means slicing a log into four, wedge-shaped pieces and then cutting from one of the flat sides of each wedge.

A PRIMER FOR SHOPPING. When you go to the local lumber yard and ask for a 2 by 4, 6′ long, you'll get a piece the *length* you asked for, but instead of being 2″ thick it will be 1⅝″, and instead of being 4″ wide, it will be 3⅝″. It's not an error nor are you being short-changed. All finished stock is referred to, dimensionally, as it was in its original, rough-sawed state. The reduction in size is due mostly to planing, which removes all rough surfaces left by sawing and which makes it possible for you to have smooth material.

When you buy 1-by-12 boards, for example, you ask for 1″ by 12″ by the length required. Again you get the length you asked for but the thickness is ¾″ or ¾″ + while the width will be reduced by as much as a half inch.

You *can* buy lumber in the rough and get every little chip you paid for—but it will require planing on your part, and few homeworkshops are equipped for this chore. Some cabinet-making shops and, of course, commercial furniture houses will buy lumber in the rough in quantity. It is a good procedure if it can be done since rough lumber will "keep" better than finished lumber. Also, with a planer on hand, you can finish lumber to the exact thickness you want.

Lumber is measured and the price figured by a unit called the "board foot," based on the actual size of the lumber in its rough-sawed state. A board foot is simply a piece of wood which measures 1″ by 12″ by 12″ or any equivalent. A piece of lumber 2″ by 6″ by 12″ is also a board foot. A piece 2″ by 12″ by 12″ is *two* board feet.

NOMINAL AND ACTUAL SIZES OF LUMBER

Nominal Size	Actual Size
1 x 2	25/32″ x 1⅝″
2 x 2	1⅝ x 1⅝
1 x 3	25/32 x 2⅝
2 x 3	1⅝ x 2⅝
1 x 4	25/32 x 3⅝
2 x 4	1⅝ x 3⅝
1 x 5	25/32 x 4⅝
1 x 6	25/32 x 5⅝
2 x 6	1⅝ x 5⅝
1 x 8	25/32 x 7½
2 x 8	1⅝ x 7½
1 x 10	25/32 x 9½
2 x 10	1⅝ x 9½
1 x 12	25/32 x 11½
2 x 12	1⅝ x 11½

Shaped pieces such as mouldings are sold by the lineal or running foot, and prices are affected by the size and the elaborateness of the design and/or the material. Laths, and shingles and shakes too, are sold by the bundle or "square"; plywood by the square foot. If you ask your dealer for the price of ¼″ or ¾″ plywood—or any available thickness for that matter—and he tells you "so much per foot," you don't have to worry about thickness since each thickness has its own price-per-foot.

Lumber yards stock lumber in standard sizes, usually starting at 8′ long and increasing by two-foot jumps up to 20′ or 24′. If your requirements call for a piece 1″ by 12″ by 7′, you can get it cut to that length, but you will probably pay for the 1′ that is cut off, unless the man explains to you that his shortest stock is 8′ long and suggests that you take the whole 8′ and saw it to length yourself so you can save the cut-off for something else.

It's wise to buy lumber in the lowest grade suitable for your purpose. Let the project, or the project component decide. It doesn't make sense to use a beautiful clear pine (which can run up to fifty cents a board foot) for storage shelves in the garage when ordinary shelving will do.

Many times, a good material in a lower grade will do for even a "good" project, especially if you don't need too much of it. This is accomplished by culling the lower grade—that is, sawing it up into pieces as big as possible or to the dimensions required, but planning the cuts so the blemishes will be discarded. Lumber can even be salvaged from crates if the project permits use of such material. Many a box or crate originally built to hold apples or oranges has been reclaimed by a practical craftsman, carefully taken apart, and made into an attractive project.

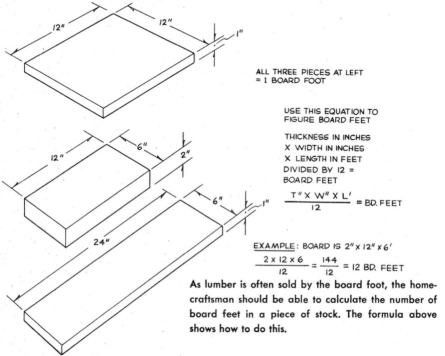

ALL THREE PIECES AT LEFT = 1 BOARD FOOT

USE THIS EQUATION TO FIGURE BOARD FEET

THICKNESS IN INCHES
X WIDTH IN INCHES
X LENGTH IN FEET
DIVIDED BY 12 =
BOARD FEET

$$\frac{T'' \times W'' \times L'}{12} = \text{BD. FEET}$$

EXAMPLE: BOARD IS 2″ x 12″ x 6′

$$\frac{2 \times 12 \times 6}{12} = \frac{144}{12} = 12 \text{ BD. FEET}$$

As lumber is often sold by the board foot, the home-craftsman should be able to calculate the number of board feet in a piece of stock. The formula above shows how to do this.

CHAPTER FIVE

PLYWOOD

MOST OF the slabs in furniture being manufactured today are plywood. The use of this material has many advantages:

1. The construction of the panel itself provides great strength plus resistance to warping and cracking.

2. The manufacturing techniques make available large panels which eliminate the need to glue up boards to make a wide piece of stock.

3. It permits the use of rare or beautiful woods which might otherwise be unavailable or prohibitively costly.

4. It can even improve on nature since the grain patterns and figures of the surface veneers can be arranged and matched for attractive effects. Blemishes and imperfections can be removed before the veneer is applied.

5. A beautiful wood which may lack the qualities needed for strong construction can still be available through its use as a plywood veneer.

HOW PLYWOOD IS MADE. Basically, plywood is a sandwich of thin sheets of wood assembled so each ply has its grain running at right angles to the next one. A five-ply panel, for example, would consist of a piece of core stock, which is usually much thicker and made from a less costly material than the other plies used. A thinner cross-banding is glued to each side of this core so its grain is at right angles to the initial piece. Two other sheets are added in a similar fashion. One of these is the face veneer, which represents the good side of the panel; the other is the back veneer, which can be a less costly material.

An initial negative reaction to plywood has long since gone and the product is acceptable today in the commercial and home manufacture of both economy designs and high-quality products. In the final analysis, care and sincerity in making the project are the major factors in quality. It is wise to remember that in pieces utilizing both plywood and solid stock, the solid wood should be of the same species and of the same quality as the face veneer of the plywood.

Veneer plies are sliced from logs which are called peelers. In the manufac-

INTERIOR-TYPE PLYWOOD

Grade-Trademark	Typical Uses	Veneer Quality[1]			Standard Stock Sizes[2]		
		FACE	BACK	INNER PLYS	Width Ft.	Length Ft.	Thickness (Inches) [3] $\frac{1}{4}$ $\frac{5}{16}$ $\frac{3}{8}$ $\frac{1}{2}$ $\frac{5}{8}$ $\frac{3}{4}$
INT-DFPA·A-A	Use indoors where both sides to be in view. Cabinet doors, built-ins, furniture.	A	A	D	3-4	8	● ● ● ● ●
INT-DFPA·A-B	Alternate for A-A. For uses requiring one surface highest appearance, opposite side solid and smooth.	A	B	D	3-4	8	● ● ● ● ●
INT-DFPA A-D DOUGLAS FIR DFPA	For interior use where high appearance of only one side is important such as paneling, built-ins and backing.	A	D	D	3-4	8	● ● ● ● ● ●
PLYFORM	Re-usable concrete form plywood. Edge sealed with distinctive green sealer. Mill oiled unless otherwise specified.	B	B	C	4	8	● ●
2·4·1	B-B utility panel. Used where two smooth sides are required.	B	B	D	4	8	● ● ● ● ●
PLYSCORD	Utility panels for uses requiring one smooth, solid side. Backing, cabinet sides, etc.	B	D	D	4	8	● ● ● ● ●
INT-DFPA B-B	Underlayment grade. Base for tile, linoleum, carpeting.	C Plugged	D	C[4] D	4	8	● ● ● ● ●
INT-DFPA B-D	Unsanded sheathing or structural grade. For sheathing, subflooring, etc., barricades.	C	D	D	4	8	● ● ● ● ●
PLYSCORD	Unsanded structural grade panel with waterproof glue line. For sheathing, subfloor, etc.	C	D	D	4	8	● ● ● ● ●
UNDERLAYMENT	New combination subfloor and underlayment base for tile, linoleum, carpeting and wood strip flooring. Used on 4-foot span grid system.	C Plugged	D	C[5] or D	4	8	7-Ply 1 $\frac{1}{8}$" Only

[1] All grades sanded both sides except C-C Exterior, Interior Plyscord and 2·4·1.

[2] Sizes other than those shown are available upon order. King size panels 12', 14', 16', 20' and longer are also available.

[3] Panels $\frac{3}{8}$" and thinner have a minimum of 3 plys; $\frac{1}{2}$" to $\frac{3}{4}$" are 5-ply minimum; thicker panels have 7-ply minimum.

[4] Veneer next to face is C or better.

[5] If face veneer thickness is less than $\frac{1}{6}$", veneer next to face C or better.

Courtesy Douglas Fir Plywood Assoc.

turing process, the peeler log is placed in what amounts to a large lathe where it revolves against a giant knife so that a continuous ribbon of wood is removed. Defective portions of the ply are removed and the remainder is cut up into practical sizes. The veneer is then dried, graded, and stacked.

Generally speaking, there is "softwood" plywood and "hardwood" plywood. These may be arbitrary designations at this point, but most plywood manufactured for construction and industrial use utilizes Douglas fir or one of twenty-three other Western softwoods. Douglas fir is the most prominent.

Hardwood plywood generally refers to plywood which has all its plies made of hardwood or just the face veneer. You can get it as "all-veneer," which, as the name implies, is construction entirely of veneers. It may be a "lumber-core" plywood, which is mostly five-ply and has a thick center-piece of solid wood. This type is usually made as a five-ply panel. Composite panels —specialty plywood—may have a core of some wood-base material such as flakeboard or particleboard with visible outer veneers of hardwood.

Wise utilization of plywood calls for some preplanning so cuts can be made with a minimum of waste and so grain direction on various components will be compatible when the project is viewed as a whole. This may be accomplished by following the main-part system described in a previous chapter of project making—planning the grain direction and cutting out the main parts first and then going on from there—or a scale plan of the panel can be penciled on paper and the parts of the project scaled onto that. This may not be too important when a utility-grade plywood is used for a painted project, but when you buy a panel of fancy hardwood that you plan to use for a natural-finish project, it can be quite critical.

VENEERING. Veneering makes it possible to extend the availability of those variations in tree formations which result in distinctive and beautiful grain patterns. For example, a board foot of bird's-eye maple won't go very far, but if it were sliced into veneer, it would cover a good-sized panel. The following is a brief discussion of other figures and patterns that are available in veneers.

Burls. The result of an injury to the growing, outer layer of certain tree cells creates a need for a protective covering in that area and causes an abnormality of growth that produces wood in knurled, uneven formations. These large, wart-like growths are cut from the tree and peeled like an apple to produce a valuable and attractive veneer.

Butts. Some sudden growth of a tree can cause the wood fibers in its base to compress, wrinkle, and twist. This writhing movement of growth traces intricate figures from which veneers can be made. "Butts" are the stumps of such trees, cross-sections of which are sliced to produce the figure. You don't get this in all wood, but of those in which it is found, walnut is the most common.

Crotch. Where a main branch leaves the trunk of the tree or where the trunk itself separates to form a fork, that's where you'll get a beautiful veneer. It's possible to imagine the twisting and wrinkling that must take place at those points to adjust to such a separation in the growth of its parts. There is also "feather crotch," which has a feather-like figure from being cut near the heart of the log; and "moon crotch," which is a result of cutting near the bark.

Some other figures and patterns are known as fiddleback, leaf, flake, blisterswirl, mottle, etc.

In addition to the design inherent in the wood itself, the method of cutting the log affects the results. Straight and quarter-sawing is seen a good deal on oak where it reveals a flake pattern. Some very hard woods which are difficult to slice may also be treated in this fashion. Ebony is an example. Rift-cutting is where the knife operates at a 45-degree angle to the rings and produces a striped effect. A back-cut is the result of a procedure that allows the heart wood to be sliced first. Half-rounding is done to yield sheets which will have a symmetrical pattern when veneered. A striped effect is produced when the log is quartered and cut at approximate right angles to the growth rings. The rotary cut peels ribbons of veneer from a lathe-mounted log.

CHAPTER SIX

COMPOSITION BOARD

HARDBOARD. Hardboard is made from wood chips which are reduced to the basic wood fibers. Then these are re-united under heat and pressure to form a panel product which is grainless, dense, and durable, and which is adaptable to many uses. There are no knots or other imperfections.

Since it is grainless, its strength runs in either direction and it can be easily worked with the same tools you use on natural lumber. It will, however, dull tools faster since it is harder and more abrasive.

Hardboard, manufactured as described and made available without additional treatment, is *standard* hardboard, widely used in construction and in

Hardboard has many uses in furniture construction . . .

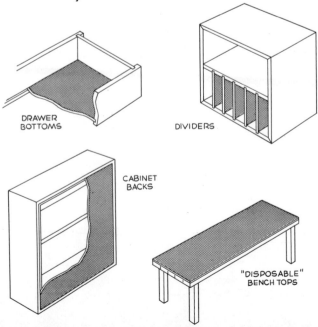

DRAWER
BOTTOMS

DIVIDERS

CABINET
BACKS

"DISPOSABLE"
BENCH TOPS

Wall, bar and sink in this project are covered with Marlite, a plastic-surfaced hardboard. Wood grain and black marble are two of a variety of surfaces available.

the fabrication of various products. Other processes result in hardboard with particular properties, such as *tempered* hardboard which, because of additional treatment and heat-treating of the standard product, takes on added hardness, stiffness, strength, and more resistance to abrasion and moisture.

You can get hardboard with one smooth side (SIS) or two smooth sides (S2S) and with a good variety of surface textures such as *striated, grooved, tiled,* and *embossed.* You're probably familiar with it in its *perforated* form. It is also available pre-finished, prime-coated and in wood-grain patterns. Panel sizes range up to 5' in width and up to 16' in length; thickness can run from ⅛" up to ¾". It has found great use as a core material over which are bonded beautiful veneers, fabrics, plastics, and other materials.

As yet, it has not achieved full utilization in home-workshop furniture construction where it seems to be limited to case backs, vertical dividers and drawer bottoms, or as a cover material such as a "disposable" workbench top.

Popular thicknesses stocked by most dealers include ⅛", ³⁄₁₆", and ¼" in both standard and tempered varieties. If you need it for indoor use, ask for the standard; for outdoor use or indoor applications where high humidity may be a factor, ask for the tempered. Like plywood, a popular sheet size is 4' by 8' but smaller panels are available.

PARTICLEBOARD. Particleboard is also a "wood" panel made by combining flakes, chips, and shavings of wood with resins and sizing compounds and then pressing them into panels. The basic wood shape in some of these may be uniform throughout while in others, depending on the process followed, the panel may actually be a ply-board with a central core of coarse flakes sandwiched between layers of fine particles to produce a smoother face-surface.

Particleboard is a relatively new material and great strides are being made to produce it or treat it in various ways to broaden its applications. For commercial use, panels are cut to size according to specifications submitted by the customer, edges are banded, surfaces are veneered, printed, embossed, etc. Many sink and bathroom vanity tops are now made by hot-roll forming laminates and then bonding them to particleboard which has been pre-shaped by fabrication or molding. Gradually, particleboard is finding its way into even more structural areas and as these increase, so will its use by the home-craftsman.

A quick look at some present-day uses may suggest applications you can utilize to advantage in your own shop and home jobs.

Biggest use at present—furniture core stock and floor underlayment. As a core stock it is used for slabs on tables, bureaus, and many other products which are basically case construction. It can be dadoed, routed, shaped, cut, etc., with the same tools used for natural wood. Like hardboard, it is abrasive and will dull tools faster but good strides have been made in making it less abrasive than it used to be.

It is being used as a core stock for wall paneling and for doors, this because its dimensional stability is good and its smooth surfaces are ideal for laminated decorative face materials. Panels have been used in a natural state, like a plywood panel, for dividers, and it is occasionally used as shelves. Recently, a particleboard product which is pierced has been introduced. Thus you have ready-made filigree panels which may be utilized for such things as room dividers, screens, accent doors, etc.

CHAPTER SEVEN

NAILS

A NAIL has holding power because wood fibers, after the nail has been driven, tend to return to their original position; thus they wedge against the nail shank. Excessively heavy hammer blows, while they will drive a nail faster, will break rather than bend the wood fibers and the nail will have less holding power. This doesn't mean that you should drive a 10d nail with a tack hammer, but it does mean that the operation shouldn't be a demonstration of strength.

Hit nails firmly; let the hammer do the job. You should be able to drive quite a few nails without feeling arm strain, without allowing the hammer head to slip off the nail and damage the wood, and without missing the nail completely. You'll be off to a good start by choosing a hammer wisely.

A hammer may have a *plain face* or a *bell face*. The plain face is easier to use because it has a flat surface. However, the bell face, which has a hitting surface that is more convex than the plain face, is a better choice since the shape lets you drive nails flush without harm to adjacent surfaces. For this reason the bell face is preferred by experienced craftsmen.

Another important factor is the weight of the hammer. They range in weight from 7 to 28 ounces; the "weight" actually being the weight of the hammer head. It's a good idea to have several sizes on hand but the one you will use most for cabinetmaking and furniture construction is the 16-ounce size.

Another factor is the "feel" of the hammer, and this is a personal thing. Be selective and choose a hammer that suits you. Test it for balance in your hand by grasping it firmly near the *end* of the handle and driving an imaginary nail. There is no doubt that when faced with an assortment of similar hammers you will be able to select a particular one simply because it feels better in your hand.

DO AND DON'TS OF NAILS AND NAILING. Select nails on the basis of appearance and length. If holding power is more important than appearance,

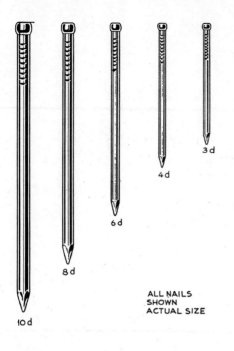

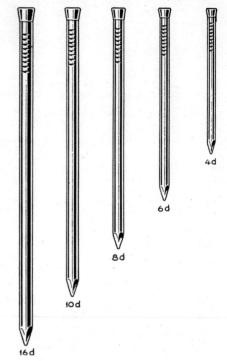

ALL NAILS
SHOWN
ACTUAL SIZE

FINISHING NAILS are used for decorative work where heads must be concealed or flush with work surface. Some have cupped heads which make them easier to countersink and cover with wood putty.

CASING NAILS are used for interior trim and cabinet work. They are slightly heavier in gauge than finishing nails but are otherwise similar.

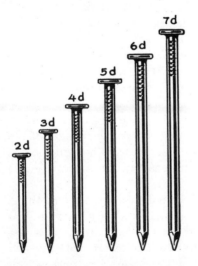

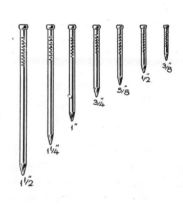

COMMON NAILS are made for general construction work where nail heads do not have to be concealed, although they can be "set" with a flat-faced punch. They come as large as 60d, which is a 6" spike.

BRADS are smaller and thinner than finishing nails and are used for light assembly where heads must be concealed. Sold by length rather than by penny sizes.

34

RECOMMENDED NAILS FOR PLYWOOD

Plywood Thickness	Type of Nail	Size
3/4"	casing	6d
	finishing	6d
5/8	finishing	6d–8d
1/2	finishing	4d–6d
3/8	finishing	3d–4d
1/4	brads	3/4"–1"
	finishing	3d
	lath	1"

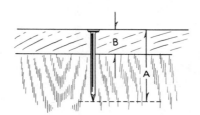

GENERAL RULE: FOR NAIL LENGTH
SELECTION - "A" SHOULD EQUAL 3("B")

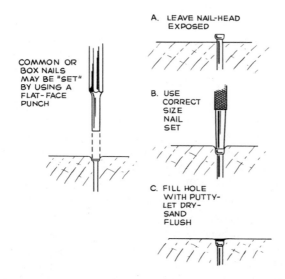

COMMON OR
BOX NAILS
MAY BE "SET"
BY USING A
FLAT-FACE
PUNCH

A. LEAVE NAIL-HEAD
     EXPOSED

B. USE
     CORRECT
     SIZE
     NAIL
     SET

C. FILL HOLE
     WITH PUTTY-
     LET DRY-
     SAND
     FLUSH

use common nails. When appearance is more important, select finishing nails since they can be set beneath the surface of the wood so they are hidden. Nail length is based on application. Generally speaking, the nail length should be three times the thickness of the face piece. For example, if were nailing through the surface of 1″ stock to attach the piece to the edge of another, the nail should be 3″ long. When face-nailing two pieces (surface-to-surface) select a nail length that will be about 3/16″ or 1/4″ less than the combined thickness of the two pieces.

Craftsman's method of hiding nails is to lift a slim shaving of wood from the nail area and then drive and set the nail in the depression. The shaving is then glued back to its original position. When neatly done, no trace of the nail is visible.

When working with finishing nails, hammer-drive the nail until the nail head is *almost* flush. Then use a nail set to finish the job. Use the right nail set; they come in sizes that range from 1/32″ up to 5/32″. Since they are not expensive, it's wise to buy a set rather than a single unit. Don't set nails deeper than 1/16″ to 1/8″.

End or edge nailing requires special care, especially when the wood has a tendency to split. Sometimes, blunting the nail by tapping the point with the hammer helps. If it doesn't, then drill small holes before driving the nails.

A lot of nails driven on the same line will almost surely split the wood. Fewer nails and staggered will spread the strain over more grain lines, will be stronger and will minimize the possibility of splitting. If a nail bends you can sometimes continue driving it if you use pliers to straighten it *at the bend*. Don't force it if it continues to bend; remove it and use another.

Use light hammer blows to start a nail and be especially careful to start it straight. Heavy grain will sometimes deflect a nail point and send it off in another direction to emerge where it's least wanted. If experience with a first few tries indicates this is likely, then take the time and trouble to drill small holes first.

CHAPTER EIGHT

SCREWS

WHEN CORRECTLY driven, screws have great holding power and, of importance in many applications, they can be removed if necessary. Another consideration of importance in furniture construction is that they pull parts together. Not only does this add to strength and rigidity but in some instances can eliminate the need for clamping. Screws can be more decorative than nails and in many applications are more acceptable exposed than nails would be.

Unless you are working with very small screws, or the material is quite soft, it is a wise procedure to drill a pilot hole to eliminate splitting and make screw-driving easier. The depth and diameter of the pilot hole are quite important since they should permit the screw to drive easily, yet not open the material to the point where the screw loses efficiency. The shank, or body hole, is always the same size—or maybe a fraction larger—than the gauge of the screw. When used, a countersink should have a diameter and a bevel angle to match the screwhead. On soft materials, the depth of the counter-

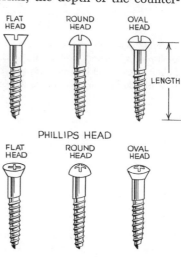

Wood screws come with flat, round, or oval heads. Flat-headed screws are usually countersunk, round- or oval-headed screws either left exposed or counterbored. Slotted screws are driven with a regular screwdriver; Phillips head screws require special Phillips screwdriver.

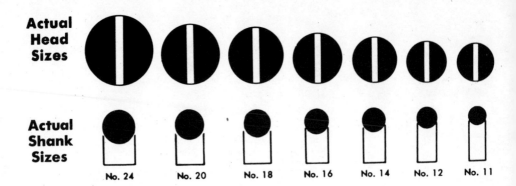

Actual Head Sizes

Actual Shank Sizes

No. 24   No. 20   No. 18   No. 16   No. 14   No. 12   No. 11

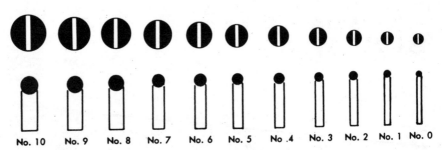

No. 10 No. 9 No. 8 No. 7 No. 6 No. 5 No .4 No. 3 No. 2 No. 1 No. 0

Actual head and shank sizes of wood screws No. 0 through No. 24. Lengths vary from ¼" to 5" depending on size.

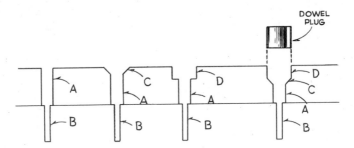

Correct method of joining two pieces of wood with screws: First, drill pilot hole (B) through both pieces. Second, drill shank, or clearance, hole (A) through top piece. Third, countersink hole if screw head is to be flush with surface. If dowel plugs are used to conceal screws, drill hole for plug (D) first. Pilot hole should be half the length of threaded portion of screw.

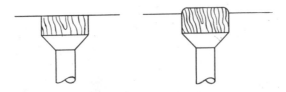

Dowel plugs may be sanded flush or allowed to project as a decorative detail. Plugs may also be made from a contrasting wood.

sink can be less than needed since taking up on the screw will sink it enough so it will be flush with adjacent surfaces. It is also true that small screws in hard woods and screws up to an inch long and as heavy as 5 gauge in soft woods can be driven very satisfactorily by using an awl or an icepick to form a starting hole. Never get a screw started by driving it part way with a hammer.

A fairly typical procedure that you might follow when using screws to hold two boards together would be as follows:

Hold the boards together under clamps or tack-nail if possible. Then lay out the screw locations. Drill the pilot hole through the first piece of wood and into the second. Enlarge the pilot hole in the first piece of wood to the shank size of the screw and then, if needed, form the countersink. It's easy to see what happens when you drive the screw. It begins to grip as it enters the second piece of wood and, during the last turn or two, it pulls the first piece down tightly against the second one.

Screwdrivers come in various sizes so it's a good idea to have an assortment on hand so you can match the blade of the screwdriver to the size of the screw. It should fit the slot in the screw-head snugly and its width at the tip should not be greater than the diameter of the screw-head. This works out

MATCHING SCREWS AND DRILL SIZES
FOR PILOT AND CLEARANCE HOLES

| Screw | Pilot Holes | | | | Clearance Holes | |
| | HARDWOODS | | SOFTWOODS | | | |
	A	B	A	B	A	B
0	$\frac{1}{32}$"	66	$\frac{1}{64}$"	75	$\frac{1}{16}$"	52
1		57	$\frac{1}{32}$	71	$\frac{5}{64}$	47
2		54	$\frac{1}{32}$	65	$\frac{3}{32}$	42
3	$\frac{1}{16}$	53	$\frac{3}{64}$	58	$\frac{7}{64}$	37
4	$\frac{1}{16}$	51	$\frac{3}{64}$	55	$\frac{7}{64}$	32
5	$\frac{5}{64}$	47	$\frac{1}{16}$	53	$\frac{1}{8}$	30
6		44	$\frac{1}{16}$	52	$\frac{9}{64}$	27
7		39	$\frac{1}{16}$	51	$\frac{5}{32}$	22
8	$\frac{7}{64}$	35	$\frac{5}{64}$	48	$\frac{11}{64}$	18
9	$\frac{7}{64}$	33	$\frac{5}{64}$	45	$\frac{3}{16}$	14
10	$\frac{1}{8}$	31	$\frac{3}{32}$	43	$\frac{3}{16}$	10
11		29	$\frac{3}{32}$	40	$\frac{13}{32}$	4
12		25	$\frac{7}{64}$	38	$\frac{7}{32}$	2
14	$\frac{3}{16}$	14	$\frac{7}{64}$	32	$\frac{1}{4}$	D
16		10	$\frac{9}{64}$	29	$\frac{17}{64}$	I
18	$\frac{13}{64}$	6	$\frac{9}{64}$	26	$\frac{19}{64}$	N
20	$\frac{7}{32}$	3	$\frac{11}{64}$	19	$\frac{21}{64}$	P
24	$\frac{1}{4}$	D	$\frac{3}{16}$	15	$\frac{3}{8}$	V

NOTE:

A = Closest size twist drill (in fractions of an inch)

B = Number or letter size drill

RECOMMENDED SCREWS FOR PLYWOOD

Plywood Thickness	Flat-Head Screws		
	screw	length	pilot hole
$\frac{3}{4}''$	#8	$1\frac{1}{2}''$	$\frac{5}{32}''$
$\frac{5}{8}$	#8	$1\frac{1}{4}$	$\frac{5}{32}$
$\frac{1}{2}$	#6	$1\frac{1}{4}$	$\frac{1}{8}$
$\frac{3}{8}$	#6	1	$\frac{1}{8}$
$\frac{1}{4}$	#4	$\frac{3}{4}$	$\frac{7}{64}$

quite logically since screwdrivers with broad, heavy tips will have longer and heavier handles so driving large screws will be easier. On the other hand, the smaller screws require more delicate screwdrivers, which makes it difficult to apply so much pressure that you run the danger of ruining the slot and even snapping the screw.

When driving a screw is difficult, even when the lead hole is correct (and this will happen in some materials), try coating the threads with soap or wax. This will make them drive more easily. If you make a mistake and drill an oversize lead hole, or if repeated removals have enlarged the hole to the point where the screw threads no longer grip tightly, you can often compensate by partially filling the hole with some steel wool or small slivers of wood. If these or similar methods don't do the trick, then change to the next size screw.

Screws can be concealed by countersinking deeper than necessary and then filling the hole with wood dough. This, however, is not the most satisfactory method. A better way is to counterbore deep enough so the screwhead will end up about ¼″ below the wood surface. Then fill the hole with a dowel. This can be sanded flush after the glue dries. If you plan much of this, it will be wise to check into getting a few plug cutters. With these you can make your own short dowels from the same material used in the project, which will make it possible to match the concealment plug to surrounding areas to the point where it will be difficult to discern.

Screws come in many materials—brass, steel, stainless steel, aluminum, galvanized or plated with chromium or cadmium, and there are screws with decorative heads. Usually, when you buy a piece of decorator hardware, you will get screws with it that will match the finish and the design of the piece.

Except for the attachment of hardware or detail components which can't be secured in other ways, most screws in furniture construction are hidden, so steel or galvanized steel screws work out quite well.

CHAPTER NINE

OTHER FASTENERS AND HARDWARE

ALTHOUGH NAILS and screws are the most common types of fasteners, there are others which can be extremely useful. All shops, for example, should maintain an assortment of corrugated nails and special fasteners which can be used on miter joints. Corrugated nails can be useful in many places where appearance is not a great factor or where the fastener will be concealed after assembly. They can be used on miters, on edge-to-edge joints, or to assemble frames with butt joints. In some instances they may set below the surface of the wood and puttied over much like a finishing nail.

A stapling gun can be a most useful shop accessory. On many jobs it can

Corrugated nails (top) and special, patented fasteners for miter joints can be used to advantage where the edge will eventually be concealed. Some types of fasteners can be set and puttied over like a nail.

A good stapling gun facilitates many operations. In this assembly of beveled pieces, the pieces can be cut slightly oversize and the staples cut off after the glue dries, or the staples can be removed and the holes filled with putty.

Tee-Nuts make it possible to have steel threads in wood. Here they are being used to mount a speaker in a hi-fi cabinet.

This cutaway shows a bolt and nut used to attach a leg. In such cases, use carriage bolts, since they have a square shank beneath the head which locks in the hole and permits tightening the nut even though you can't reach the head.

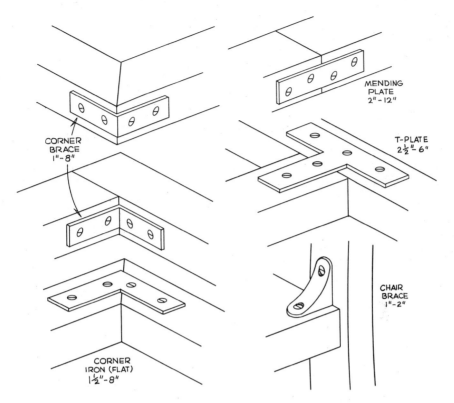

CORNER
BRACE
1"-8"

MENDING
PLATE
2"-12"

T-PLATE
2½"-6"

CHAIR
BRACE
1"-2"

CORNER
IRON (FLAT)
1½"-8"

Various types of metal fastening hardware are available for reinforcing joints. Sometimes they can be used for the entire assembly.

Handi-Brackets can be used to create hangers, stands, etc., and to reinforce furniture. They range in size from 1" to 4" high, take No. 9 wood screws or 3/16" bolts or rivets.

substitute for a hammer. On other occasions it can be used as a tacking medium. And don't overlook the use of staples as a means of holding parts together until clamps can be applied. The gun should be a heavy-duty type and should be able to drive staples of different lengths. Some typical applications: attachment of cloth coverings, securing case backs, upholstery work, chair-seat coverings and pads, light picture frames and so on.

New items for fastening are being introduced constantly. Tee-Nuts provide steel threads in wood and are useful for demountable attachments as well as permanent assemblies. Jack-Nuts can provide for attachment of parts to, for example, hollow-core doors.

"Fastening hardware" includes those items known as corner irons, corner braces, mending plates, T-plates, etc. These can be obtained in different metals and finishes. Often, they do the entire assembly job; other times they are used as reinforcement. There is no stigma attached to using them for the strength they provide. This negative feeling is due, most likely, to the fact that items like this are often used to do repair work or on assemblies with joints so simple they lack strength in themselves. But don't let this influence you into ignoring them.

Other pieces of fastening hardware are made for a very special purpose. Typical would be a chair or table corner-brace. This is just a shaped piece of steel through which you can pass a lag screw into the inside corner of a leg. Taking up on the screw locks leg and rails firmly together.

These are some of the types of fastening hardware that are available to the modern home workshopper. Look for new items by making regular trips to well-stocked hardware stores.

CHAPTER TEN

GLUES AND CLAMPING

GREAT STRIDES have been made in adhesives—to the point where it is safe to say that quality construction no longer has to rely entirely on intricate joinery. A typical example of great and gratifying progress is the method used today to laminate a cover material to a slab—for example, Formica to a counter top. You don't use glue and weights, and therefore eliminate all the accompanying time-consuming and frustrating procedures. You merely brush on a *contact cement,* in a few minutes apply the material, and it's done—actually ready for the next step in the construction procedure.

Now this is a rather quick picture and it's not meant to imply that modern adhesives are cure-alls or that they permit such haste that it leads to carelessness or loose-fitting parts. There are still rules to follow, and the most important ones are these:

1. Preparation of the surfaces to be bonded is important since neglect here can cause a weak joint if not outright failure. Mating areas should be thoroughly dusted after sanding. Hard, dense surfaces will glue better if they are roughened slightly by some sanding across the grain.

2. Apply glue carefully to avoid staining adjacent surfaces. Glue squeezed out of a joint under clamping pressure should be wiped off immediately with a damp cloth. If the glue is allowed to remain, it will seal the wood and prevent stain penetration. If you allow it to dry before removing it, you'll have a rough sanding job on hand.

3. Glue does have body, which is one reason why joints should not fit so tightly they must be forced into place. This is especially true of fittings like the mortise-tenon and dowel joints. The ends of tenons should be chamfered to allow some room for excess glue. Dowels should be grooved or you can buy the ready-made type which are spiraled. Thus when the dowel is pushed into the hole, the groove, or the spiral, permits the escape of excess glue and air. A tight-fitting dowel joint without the escape provision can force glue out elsewhere or can create so much pressure that the stock will split.

4. Some woods like lemonwood, teak, even varieties of pine can contain

oil or pitch. This will leave a surface film that will prevent a good gluing job. Sometimes the bond appears to hold—until you put some pressure on it. Then it parts as if you had used saliva instead of glue. In cases like this, clean the surfaces carefully and use a casein glue.

5. Never use anything but your fingers to tighten clamps. Excessive pressure can squeeze out too much of the glue. On the other hand, you don't want to clamp so lightly that you get no "squeeze-out" at all. If clamping pressure is okay and no glue is squeezed out, it is a pretty good sign that you haven't applied enough or that there is a sloppy area in the joint and a gap or chamber where the glue can collect.

6. Most times, and this is especially true of porous materials, both mating surfaces should be glue-coated. To some extent this will depend on the product being used so this is another valid reason for reading labels and following directions.

There are "filler-type" glues; these having sufficient body or a particular additive that enables them to compensate somewhat for a poor fit. Usually, a heavy application to both surfaces is advised with some free drying time before the parts are mated but, again, follow the manufacturer's instructions.

7. Most glues are best applied by brush since this permits full and uniform application. On broad surfaces you can get good coverage by using a toothed spreader. One good trick for many uses is to thread a length of ½" rope through a short piece of tubing until it projects about 1" from one end. Unravel this end and use it to spread glue. To renew the end, all you have to do is snip off the used portion and pull out another inch of the rope.

8. Never put a joint under stress until you have allowed sufficient drying time. Some glues will set faster than others but few are ready to take strain immediately. Setting time can sometimes be pushed but never in a way that ignores instructions. The setting time of urea-resin glue can be speeded up by applying some heat to the joint. For some projects a heat-lamp is practical. Glue should not be applied to very cold surfaces nor should the glue itself be cold to the extent that it doesn't run freely.

MODERN ADHESIVES

Liquid Resin. This glue is white and is most often seen in white, plastic squeeze bottles. It has a fast setting-time, particularly at higher temperatures, is moisture resistant and, in addition to wood, will bond a variety of materials such as plastic, cork, or leather. This is a good, easy-to-use, general-purpose shop glue.

Resorcinol. A two-part product, this glue is one part powder, the other being a catalyst. It's very strong and completely waterproof so it's an excellent selection for outdoor furniture, boats, and other items that must hold together after frequent wettings. The powder and the catalyst must be mixed in the proportions suggested by the manufacturer, and you should not mix more than you need for the job on hand.

Powdered Resin. While the proportions may be altered a little, this glue usually works best by using two parts of the resin to one or ½ part of water.

Glue-coated edges should be pulled up tight enough so a thin bead of glue is squeezed out along each joint line. Too much pressure will merely remove more of the glue and "starve" the joint. Note the homemade clamping fixture.

C-clamps are made in various sizes and can be quite useful in woodworking. Be sure to use scrap pieces to protect the work.

Notched-bar clamps are simple and easy to use. They can be purchased in sizes ranging in opening capacity from 2' to 8'.

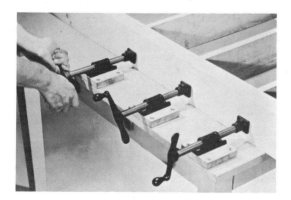

This type of press screw may be attached anywhere to solve a clamping problem, or to create a jig for repeat clamping of similar assemblies to speed the work.

These are fixed-head I-beam bar clamps and pipe clamps which are made by buying the fixtures and using them on ordinary pipes to make a clamp of any length.

Here is an example of how a set of hinged bar clamps can be attached to a bench surface to create a jig. Similar assemblies can pass through and be held firmly for either nailing or gluing.

Wooden pony-bar cabinet clamps are used on fine work where a lot of pressure is not required. As the wooden bar is unlikely to harm finished surfaces, this type of clamp is used widely for exacting repair work.

Two kinds of handscrews are available. The adjustable type permits the jaws to be set at various angles to suit the work; the nonadjustable has jaws which remain practically parallel.

It's a strong glue, light in color, excellent for furniture construction and, since it's almost waterproof, it is good to use for anything that might be subjected to dampness. A disadvantage is that you must mix it yourself.

Powdered Casein. A good glue for general woodworking, this is *the* glue to use on lemonwood, teak, and other woods which contain oil. Don't use it on oak or maple since it can stain these species. While it is moisture resistant, it is not waterproof. The powder must be mixed with an equal part of water before use and must be used, after mixing, within a specified amount of time.

Animal Glue (flake form). A good woodworking glue, it is viscous enough to fill slight cracks and gaps. Because it must be dissolved in water (in particular proportions which make it better for softwoods or hardwoods) and used hot, it is not found too often in the homeworkshop.

Animal and Fish Glue (Liquid). A very strong glue which was very popular before more modern, quicker-setting glues became available. It should be warmed to about 70 degrees before use and should be allowed to become tacky after being applied to both surfaces.

Epoxy Glues. These have not been developed to the point where they are practical for use in homeworkshop furniture construction. Unless you have a particular bonding problem, it's better to stick to one of the other adhesives described. This may change at any time. In fact it shouldn't be too long before a glue will be developed which will have an almost immediate setting-time and which will pull parts together and so eliminate the need for clamping.

Contact Cement. Not a "joint glue," although there may be times when its use in such a manner is practical. At present, it is generally used for laminat-

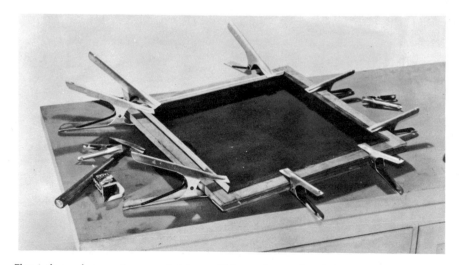

These clamps have spring-operated jaws which can be used to hold almost any material. Fast to use, they are fine for holding parts temporarily while you secure them or even for small glue jobs.

Improvised setup for clamping irregular work. The "clamp" consists of two hardwood bars, two nuts and bolts and a couple of lengths of line.

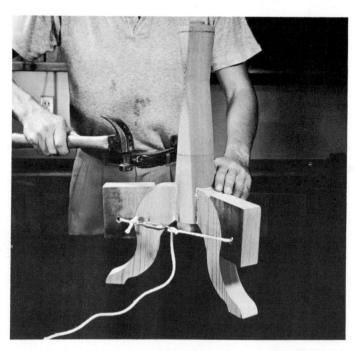

Another improvised setup that facilitates a tough gluing job. Scrap blocks are placed against the legs after being drilled to permit passage of the line. A turnbuckle pulls the line taut; tapping down on the blocks presses the legs squarely against the post.

ing jobs and in such applications it is a boon to homecraftsmen. General instructions are to coat both surfaces with a thin, uniform coating. On porous surfaces, allow the first coat to dry, then apply a second. Don't make contact until the material has dried. Best way to check for this is to press a small piece of wrapping paper against the coating. If the paper doesn't stick, you can feel free to proceed. Contact cement gets its name from the fact that it does bond on contact. Once the coated parts are mated you can't move them so care must be taken to place parts correctly. On large sheets use wrapping paper between; then when the parts are lined up, pull the wrapping paper away.

CLAMPS. Few of the projects you make would hang together for long if it were not for the fact that clamps can be used to hold the parts until the adhesive dries. Nails and screws and fastening hardware can be used, of course, but this is not always practical or compatible with quality craftsmanship. So— clamps are in order.

There are different types of clamps; so many, in fact, that it can be discouraging because each type does a particular job especially well and a large assortment of clamps can run into money. But don't despair, because a basic assortment can take you a long way. You can "make do" with clamps you already have, you can add to your set by making your own, and you can improvise along some of the lines shown in the photos.

Even if money is in great supply it's not wise to buy clamps just to fill a cabinet, because it *is* possible to buy types that you will never really have use for or which you will require so infrequently you'd be better off improvising on those occasions.

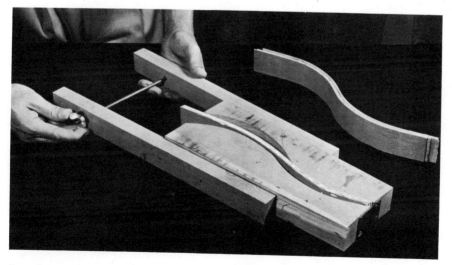

Curved components can be shaped by laminating thin strips which are easily bent. The clamping fixture has matching, curved blocks which are preshaped to the line required. Taking up on the wing nut shapes the pieces and holds them together until the glue sets.

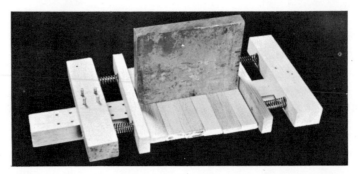

Another example of a homemade clamping device, this time for light-duty work. The springs supply the pressure for edge-gluing. The steel block is used merely to hold the pieces flat.

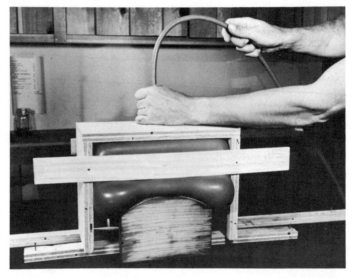

An example of how you can improvise to provide clamp action in odd situations. An air-filled balloon will conform to contours, and since the balloon is captive, great force can be exerted on the work.

Do become familar with different types so you can choose your first purchases in line with the majority of jobs you will be doing regularly. There are many types of bar clamps, some made with fixtures that can't be removed so the length of span is limited by the length of the bar. It may be better to buy fixtures which can be used on ordinary galvanized pipe. Thus, with several sets of fixtures and an assortment of pipe lengths, you can suit the clamp to the job.

You can exert great pressure with a clamp so don't use more than hand-pressure to tighten them. Pounding with a hammer or increasing leverage by using a length of pipe on the handle is forbidden. If you don't damage or bend the clamp itself you will certainly mar the work. If ever excessive pressure is needed to draw parts together it will be wise to assume that the pieces do not fit as they should.

**Part Three—FURNITURE
COMPONENTS**

CHAPTER ELEVEN

BROAD SURFACES—SLABS

FOR OUR purposes let's consider that any broad surface is a slab. A frame with an inserted panel can be a slab. Certainly desk tops, table tops, chest tops may be called slabs. Even doors and horizontal and vertical dividers may fall into such a category. Some projects may be composed entirely of slabs.

A slab may be plywood. It may be solid lumber—a large piece made by edge-gluing separate pieces of stock. It may be a framed plywood-panel or a plywood-panel inserted into two vertical posts. Or, a flush door—solid or hollow-core—is a ready-made slab. The choice of which to use depends on many factors.

Slabs are the basic components of most pieces of furniture . . .

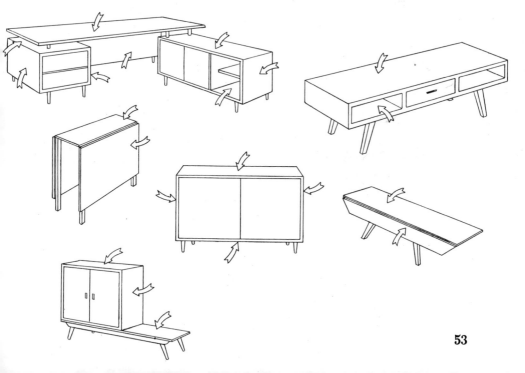

A slab may be glued-up lumber, a plywood panel, a framed plywood panel, or a flush door . . .

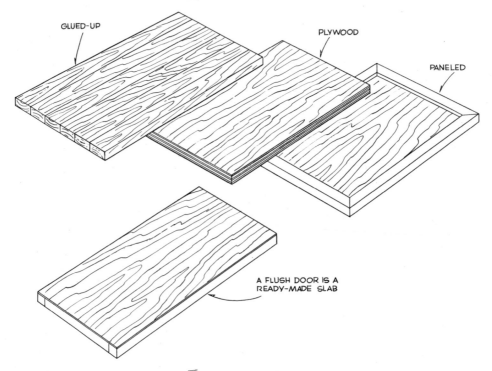

GLUED-UP

PLYWOOD

PANELED

A FLUSH DOOR IS A
READY-MADE SLAB

A 4'-by-8' sheet of plywood can be cut up into various-sized slabs to suit a particular project. Plywood can be obtained in various thicknesses from any lumber-yard dealer. This is not true of lumber. You'll find 1″ and 2″ stock anywhere, but ask for some ½″ or ¼″ lumber and chances are, if you insist on having it, it will have to be planed down for you at additional cost.

You can always gain, time-wise, by choosing plywood over lumber if for no other reason than the fact that plywood comes ready to cut up. Before you can size lumber slabs you'll have to go through the preliminaries of creating the slab.

But no one can deny the appeal of solid lumber. Even today, when there is little of the negative reaction that first greeted plywood, the connotations of the term "solid lumber" are considerable. One associates the use of the pure and whole material with loving and careful craftsmanship. On the other hand, it may also be a blind, for a solid-lumber project may be as inferior—both in construction quality and materials—as any project made from any other material.

Chances are that with most projects you will work with both plywood and lumber and possibly some other slab material such as hardboard or particleboard. When combining materials be sure that the end result is harmonious. In some areas this is not so critical. A case back does not have

To use plywood panels most efficiently and most economically, cut cardboard pieces to represent the various parts of the project and plan the cuts beforehand on paper. Now is the time to plan grain direction and to utilize fully the entire panel.

Here is how the components of a desk would be laid out on a 4-by-8 plywood panel to assure maximum use of the material and consistent grain direction.

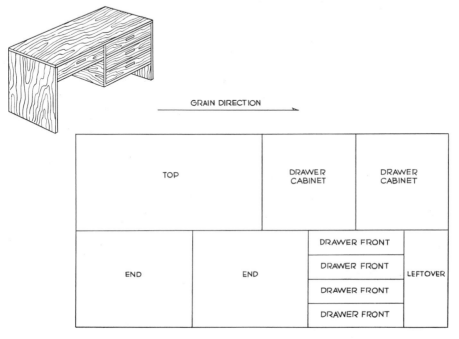

GRAIN DIRECTION →

TOP		DRAWER CABINET	DRAWER CABINET
END	END	DRAWER FRONT	
		DRAWER FRONT	LEFTOVER
		DRAWER FRONT	
		DRAWER FRONT	

You can use plywood slabs to construct a solid frame . . .

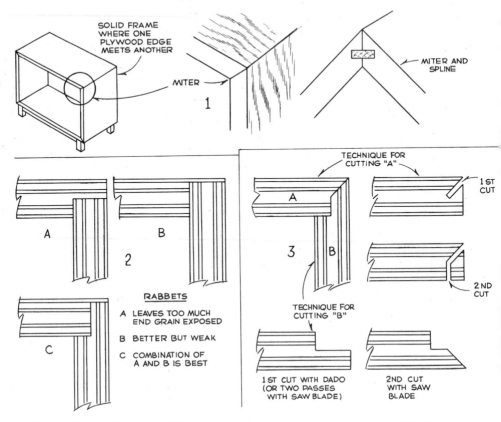

Frame of plywood slabs should be constructed using joints that are strong and hide the edge grain. 1. Miter joint, and miter with spline for added strength, leaves no edge at all. 2. Rabbet joint C is strong and conceals edge by leaving thin veneer covering on one piece. 3. Combination miter and rabbet requires two cuts on table saw on each edge, but this treatment results in a strong, neat joint in which no edges show.

to match the surface veneer or the solid-lumber material of the case top. Drawer bottoms and dust panels, and certainly cleats and glue blocks, do not have to match the materials used in visible areas.

PLYWOOD. We've already talked about the many advantages of plywood as a slab material. But are there disadvantages? Some, but in the over-all picture they become slight and can be completely minimized by proper handling of the material during cutting and construction and by knowledge of correct techniques and procedures.

The impact of the most beautiful piece of plywood can be lost because of insufficient attention to grain direction. It's a problem only if you are too anxious to cut. Make grain-direction planning a preliminary to any plywood construction job, and this takes us back to the main-part system of fabrication

Or use corner posts in various ways to achieve the same end . . .

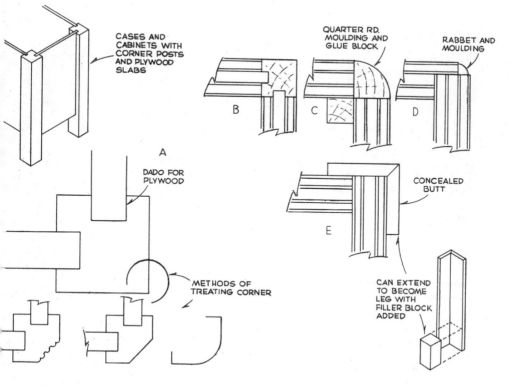

CASES AND CABINETS WITH CORNER POSTS AND PLYWOOD SLABS

QUARTER RD. MOULDING AND GLUE BLOCK

RABBET AND MOULDING

A

B

C

D

DADO FOR PLYWOOD

CONCEALED BUTT

E

METHODS OF TREATING CORNER

CAN EXTEND TO BECOME LEG WITH FILLER BLOCK ADDED

A. Corner posts can be dadoed to receive plywood; the corner can be treated decoratively.
B. Corner post flush with slab is dadoed, edge of plywood is mortised. C. Glue block on inside of frame stiffens joint, quarter-round moulding acts as corner post and conceals edges.
D. Rabbet joint and moulding creates a novel corner. E. Simple butt joint can be concealed with L-shaped strip.

and to the wood or cardboard model suggestion. A basic mock-up can be disassembled into its various parts and these in turn can be placed on a scaled plan of the plywood panel or panels. This gives you the opportunity to move the pieces around to obtain a compatible grain-direction and to plan the plywood area for each piece. It's easy—and economical—to do it first. Not so after parts are cut and you are suddenly faced with drawer fronts that have grain running in all directions.

Prominent grain can even have an effect on the visual size of a project. Run the grain vertically, and the project looks taller; run it horizontally and it looks shorter. A desk top looks longer when the grain of the top slab runs parallel to the front edge.

Working with Plywood. The face veneer on a sheet of plywood can be as thin as $\frac{1}{32}''$—even less. So it requires some care when handling and cutting. Saw blades, straight or circular, cut on the *down* stroke, except in the case of the sabre saw, which usually cuts on the *up* stroke. When using circular

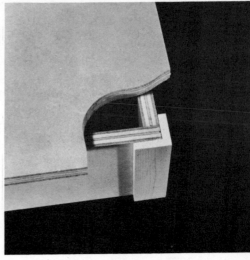

Solid wood insets, used with glue-block backing, produce corners that are both distinctive and strong. The insets may be square or triangular, round or cove. Recessed or raised insets will heighten the decorative effect.

L-shaped strip will conceal a simple butt joint. If you use a filler block for strength at the bottom, the strip could be extended and become the leg of the table. This also gives you an unbroken line from the table top to bottom of the leg.

Plywood panel inserted in a frame can also serve as a slab . . .

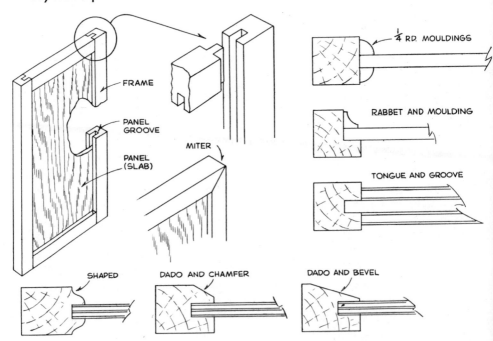

FRAME

PANEL GROOVE

PANEL (SLAB)

MITER

SHAPED

DADO AND CHAMFER

DADO AND BEVEL

¼ RD. MOULDINGS

RABBET AND MOULDING

TONGUE AND GROOVE

Framed panel eliminates problem of plywood edges. Panel can be fitted to frame in several ways, and frame can be treated decoratively with mouldings or by shaping.

HOW TO DEAL WITH THE PROBLEM OF EXPOSED PLYWOOD EDGES

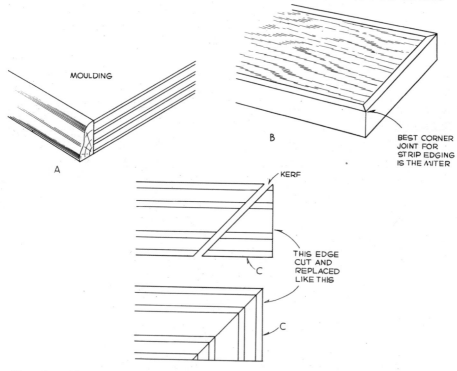

Shaped mouldings (A) or flat strips (B) can be used to conceal edges. Clever trick is to saw triangular block from edge of panel, reverse and glue it so bottom side (C) becomes edge.

Four ways to treat plywood edges (from top): solid wood strip; triangular piece cut from the plywood itself; commercial or homemade moulding that conceals the edge and bulks it; simple bevel cut to put the plies below the line of sight.

You can bulk a plywood edge and conceal the plies in several ways (from top): double the plywood thickness by gluing a strip to the underside and then banding both; insert the slab in a dado cut in solid material; set the slab in a rabbet cut in solid wood.

PLYWOOD EDGES (con't.)

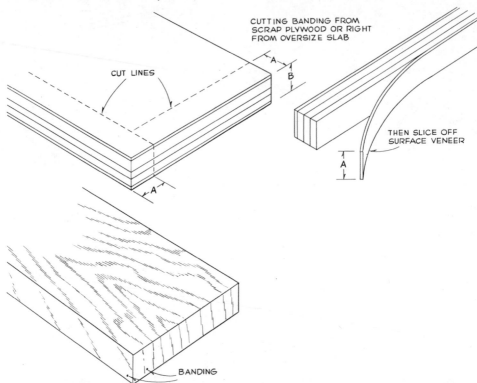

CUTTING BANDING FROM SCRAP PLYWOOD OR RIGHT FROM OVERSIZE SLAB

CUT LINES

THEN SLICE OFF SURFACE VENEER

BANDING

Waterfall effect of continuous grain running over the edges of slab can be achieved by cutting your own banding from scrap plywood or an oversized slab.

Apply banding with contact cement, but first be sure plywood edges are smooth and square. Often it is effective to cut the banding a bit wider than the edge, then sand it flush after application. Rolls of banding sold in hardware stores are 1″ wide.

blades, the *down* action would be in the direction of rotation. To minimize splintering and feathering always place the material so the cutting action is *down* through the face veneer, not *up*.

With a hand saw, place the material with the face side up. With a portable cut-off saw or a sabre saw, place the material with its face side down. When working with a table saw, radial-arm saw, jigsaw, or bandsaw, place the material with its face side up.

When working with circular blades (table saw or radial-arm saw) be sure the blade is correctly aligned, or rather, that the machine's components are aligned with the blade. If, for example, the rip fence on a table saw is not as it should be, the "back" teeth of the blade will be hitting the side of the kerf already formed by the "front" teeth and this may ruin the work.

Use sharp blades and, if at all possible, get yourself a special plywood-cutting saw blade for power tools. A good blade of this type will leave clean, splinterless corners and an edge so smooth it will not require sanding. Lacking this, use a fine crosscut blade; the more teeth the better. A hollow-ground blade will do a good job but will not hold up too long under the abrasive action of the many glue lines in plywood. Don't use a rip blade for plywood.

Handle plywood carefully to avoid the need for excessive sanding. It doesn't take much time for a modern sander, especially the belt type, to go through $\frac{1}{32}$ of an inch. Try to limit all sanding to what can be done efficiently with a pad sander, preferably with a straight-line action.

Concealing Edges. Since plywood is a multi-layered wood panel, you'll have to contend with edges that are not too attractive, but this is a characteristic of the material and it's not difficult to get around. The edges of a plywood panel which is inserted in posts or in frames are automatically concealed. Joints can be selected that will conceal the edges as well as supply strength. When the edge is neither inserted nor concealed with a joint, it may be banded with strips you can cut yourself or that you can buy. Solid wood strips can be used to bulk an edge as well as conceal the plies.

On painted jobs it is permissible to live with the edges so long as you do a good job of filling, sanding, and sealing. The paint will cover adequately. And there is always the off-beat method of leaving the plies exposed even under a natural finish, but this is acceptable only with a high-grade plywood that will reveal smooth edges free of holes and other imperfections.

CORES. Cores enter the area of slabs in the sense that a broad surface forms the base for the lamination of other materials. This could very well be a complete slab project which is then covered with another material such as plastic sheeting, Formica, etc. The construction principles of the cores are no different than those already described for plywood and solid-lumber slabs, nor do you have to seek further for ready-made cores than the products described in a previous section—products like hardboard and particleboard.

Where a base or a core is required it makes sense to choose from among plywood, hardboard, or particleboard. Going through the procedure of assembling a slab of solid lumber for this purpose is not practical.

FLUSH DOORS MAKE READY-MADE SLABS FOR TABLES, DESK TOPS

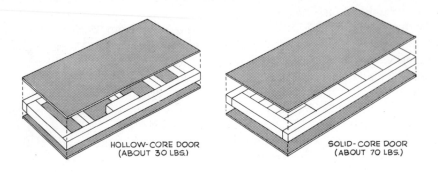

HOLLOW-CORE DOOR
(ABOUT 30 LBS.)

SOLID-CORE DOOR
(ABOUT 70 LBS.)

Hollow-core door contains spaced braces; solid-core door is filled with solid lumber. Doors come in lengths of 6'8" and 7', widths of 1'6" up to 4'.

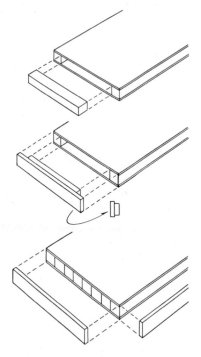

Three methods of finishing flush doors that have been reduced in size. Bottom door is solid-core type; other two are hollow cores. Edge treatment suggested for plywood also applies to flush doors.

Flush Doors. You can buy flush doors with fancy hardwood surfaces or you can buy utility types with sturdy but economical facing materials intended for painting. You can choose from facing materials such as fir, ash, maple, birch, mahogany, pine, hardboards, etc. Doors can run from 80" to 84" in length and anywhere from 18" to 48" in width. Choose a size which can be used as is or which comes closest to the slab dimensions you have in mind.

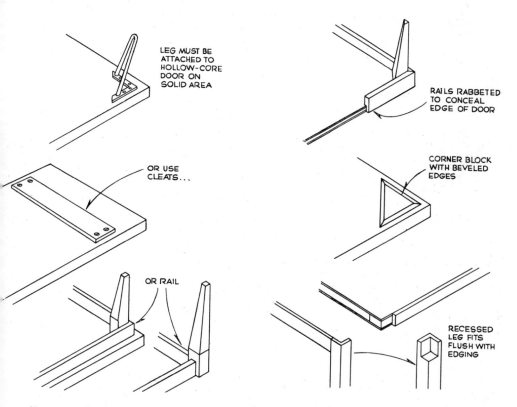

LEG MUST BE ATTACHED TO HOLLOW-CORE DOOR ON SOLID AREA

RAILS RABBETED TO CONCEAL EDGE OF DOOR

OR USE CLEATS...

CORNER BLOCK WITH BEVELED EDGES

OR RAIL

RECESSED LEG FITS FLUSH WITH EDGING

Here are a few suggestions for attaching legs to a hollow-core door. Because screws do not hold in the hollow areas, legs must either be attached to solid sections or to cleats or corner blocks which are screwed to the solid frame.

The frame construction—the inner skeleton to which are bonded the face materials—of most flush doors is basically the same; solid peripheral construction with strategically placed, solid blocks for installation of door hardware. But what is done within the area of the frame makes the difference between a "hollow-core" door and a "solid-core" door.

The solid-core door is filled in with solid lumber; the hollow-core is not, but it may contain a system of bracing or a pattern of grid-work designed to prevent warpage and add strength and rigidity.

What this means to the home furniture builder is this—

The hollow-core door is usually cheaper and can be 30 to 40 pounds lighter, but you've got to be careful about where you attach other components; a screw that is driven so it grips only the surface plywood is not going to grip too long. If you are using such a door for a table top, for example, the only practical place for leg attachment would be the outer edges where the solid framing is. Two ways to get around this: use a leg-and-rail assembly or use cleats across the width of the door to provide continuous solid material.

A hollow-core door can be cut up into smaller slabs but it does present the not-insurmountable problem of filling in the resultant gap.

You can attach anything, anywhere to a solid core door and it can be sliced up into smaller slabs quite easily.

GLUED-UP SLABS OF SOLID LUMBER ARE STRONG, ATTRACTIVE

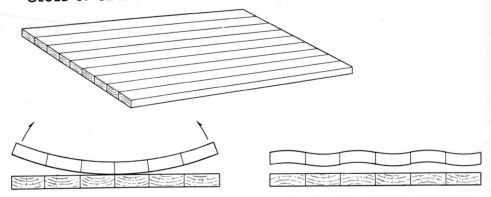

When gluing up boards to make a slab, alternate end grain of each board (right) so warping is confined to individual boards. (Warping is exaggerated in drawing.) After finishing with sander or planer, slab will be flat and smooth. If end grain of each board faces in same direction (left), warping is cumulative and affects the entire slab.

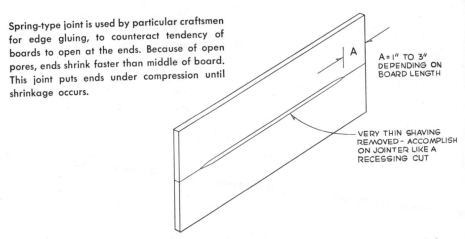

Spring-type joint is used by particular craftsmen for edge gluing, to counteract tendency of boards to open at the ends. Because of open pores, ends shrink faster than middle of board. This joint puts ends under compression until shrinkage occurs.

A

A = 1" TO 3"
DEPENDING ON
BOARD LENGTH

VERY THIN SHAVING
REMOVED - ACCOMPLISH
ON JOINTER LIKE A
RECESSING CUT

Since laminations can be seen at the edges, both hollow-core and solid-core doors should be given the same considerations afforded plywood when it comes to treating exposed edges.

SOLID LUMBER. Wide pieces of solid lumber are usually built up by gluing together comparatively narrow strips. There are two important reasons for this: Wide boards are rare and would be expensive. The widest boards you are likely to find in a local lumber yard would be 12". The second reason is, wide boards are more likely to warp than narrow ones. You must know from experience that even a 12" board can distort considerably; sometimes to the

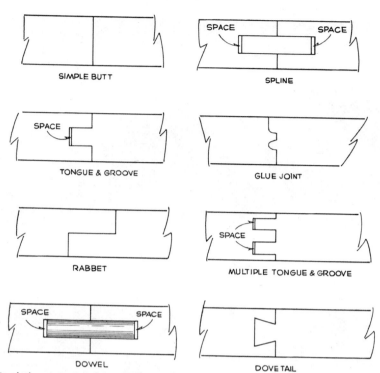

SIMPLE BUTT

SPLINE

SPACE   SPACE

TONGUE & GROOVE

SPACE

GLUE JOINT

RABBET

MULTIPLE TONGUE & GROOVE

SPACE

SPACE   SPACE

DOWEL

DOVETAIL

The simple butt joint (top left) is adequate for most edge-gluing work, but for added strength and tighter fit, you can choose from any of these other joints. The dowel joint is favored by many because of its simplicity and holding power.

Ends of glued-up slab should be concealed for attractive finish. A. Tongue-and-groove joint in solid stock. B. Simple banding, similar to technique used for plywood. C. Solid insert for a decorative pattern. D. Raised lip, perhaps for a coffee table. E. Beveled edge hides joints beneath line of sight.

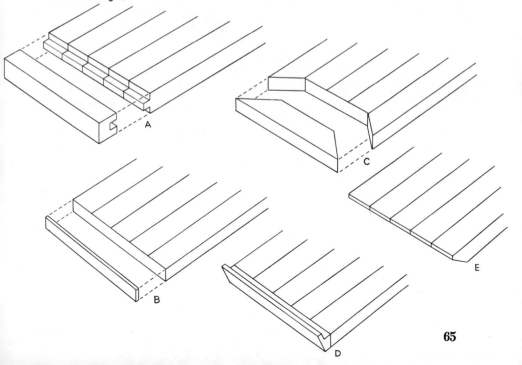

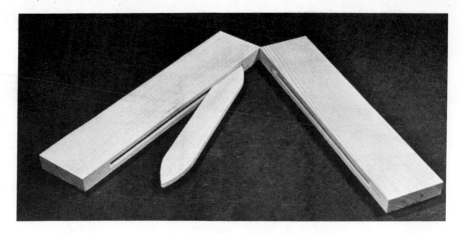

Heavy spline makes a good edge joint for gluing up stock. Note the boat shape of the spline, to conform to the arc left by the saw blade when cutting the groove.

Heavy slab of glued-up stock, which might be used for a workbench top, can be strengthened considerably with a bolt or a threaded rod with a washer and nut at each end. Holes are bored through individual boards before gluing.

point where it becomes impractical to use it as is. So, of necessity and for good craftsmanship, you glue up narrow boards to make wide ones.

Here is a simple example of how to balance the stresses in a glued-up slab and thus eliminate or minimize the chances for distortion. Take a 12″ board and rip it into three equal widths. Then take the center piece and invert it, and edge-glue the three pieces back into a solid slab. What this does is alternate the direction of the annual rings from piece to piece; thus the stresses oppose each other to balance out instead of cooperating to cause warpage. This is a typical procedure and should be followed regardless of the width of the individual pieces or of the ultimate width of the slab.

At the same time, give attention to the grain pattern. Place pieces loosely together and study the effect. They can be moved or shifted end-wise. This will also determine which will be the face side of the slab. With the decision made, draw a light pencil line across the pieces and number each one. This will establish position and order.

The ends of the boards, with their open pores, will have more tendency to shrink than the center. To combat this, a slim shaving is taken from the edges that will be glue-coated. This "spring-type" joint puts the ends of the boards under compression so that eventual shrinkage at those points won't result in distortion. It also results in a very thin glue line. It's a procedure for particular craftsmen but it should not be overdone. The shaving removed should be very fine and is best accomplished with a sharp hand-plane. See drawing for more details.

Boards for edge-gluing should be trim and square before gluing. Don't depend on clamps to pull pieces into alignment since this will only create stresses which may eventually cause joint-gaps and other unpleasant faults.

The joint you use does not have to be fancy. The drawings show many possibilities and each of these is especially suitable for a particular application, but for general work the dowel joint is always a good bet. Be sure to use dowels which are grooved or spiraled and which will fit easily in the holes drilled for them. There must be opportunity for the escape of excess glue and trapped air.

Clamping pressure should be sufficient to bring the edges into firm contact. Use a damp cloth to remove squeezed-out glue immediately; this, to avoid staining the wood but also so you can examine the joints for tightness. Clamping pressure should be uniform over the length of the slab. If possible, use clamps every 10" or 12" and alternate them over and under the work. To keep the work flat, use cleats across the surface and clamp these also.

The drawings show methods which can be used to hide the exposed grain at slab-ends. Many of the techniques described for banding, bulking, framing, and joining plywood slabs also apply to solid slab construction.

CHAPTER TWELVE

LEGS

FURNITURE LEGS can be simple or complex. They can be straight, turned, or shaped. They can be ready-mades which are simply screw-attached to the underside of a flush door or they can be the extension of a post beyond the bottom of an inserted panel, a construction that is often found on the side components of a chest. But they do have one thing in common—they support the weight of the project plus the weight of people and/or items which are stored in or on the project.

Often, and we're thinking very basically now, the leg is a means of establishing a functional height for the main part of the project; for example, table tops and seat pads. To take another point of view, leg height can be affected by more prosaic considerations. For example, you don't want to make the legs on a chest so short that the housewife can't get under it with dust mop or vacuum cleaner.

Legs are strongest (and easiest to attach) when they are vertical. The more slant they have, the more stress that is put on the attachment joint and the stronger it should be. Of course, strong joints plus stretchers will permit considerable slant, but the fact that good engineering can make it practical merely means that basic rules can be ignored occasionally if necessary. Generally, it is a good idea to limit slant to a maximum of 15 degrees, and to use this on low items such as coffee tables.

Some legs will take more of a beating than others—even on the same project. In most chairs, for example, the load is greatest over the back legs, especially when the sitter tilts the chair back. In areas such as this, the slant consideration becomes even more important. Often you can create a visual impression of slant by making taper cuts on the inside edges of straight legs, thereby combining the strength of a vertical leg with the appearance of a slanted one.

LEG DESIGN. To simplify the business of leg design and even leg styling, think of the ultimate shape as being a variation or modification of a basic form. A cross-section of the form could be circular, oval, square, rectangular, triangular. A longitudinal cut through the center of a leg could reveal one, several, or all of these shapes; the latter being especially true of turned legs. Even the shape of the cabriole leg will be easier to visualize if you picture it encased in a basic block. A head-on view of two adjacent sides would reveal duplicate contours.

Almost any power tool can play a part in leg-shaping. Tapers can be formed on a jointer or the tool can be used for stock reduction in a prescribed area. Such a reduction on two adjacent sides and for most of the length of a square would produce a shape with Oriental styling. The table saw will cut square legs and with a special jig can produce tapers. With a moulding head it can do some fluting and reeding; with a dado head (or a moulding head and blank knives) it can be used to reduce stock.

The bandsaw is necessary to produce cabriole shapes and, when size permits, the jigsaw can serve in the same capacity. The lathe is necessary for turned forms and sometimes serves an accessory role for additional details on a form shaped on another machine—a turned club foot on a cabriole leg is one example.

Sometimes a machine is used merely to create a raw form, after which additional shaping, carving, detailing, finishing, etc., are done by hand.

Leg shape does much to establish the style of a piece. When making a reproduction you have no choice but to copy. When making original pieces you can simplify leg production by keeping shapes and forms in line with your ambitions, your likes and dislikes in woodworking procedures, and your equipment. If you don't own a lathe, or merely tolerate lathe work, don't, for example, attempt to build a set of dining-room furniture that involves round legs and arms and spindle backs. Think of the turning required to make six or eight chairs! You can get around such situations by buying "ready-mades," but we'll discuss that in the next section.

To carry the thought of variations on a basic form a bit further, let's consider a cylinder. Used as is, it is a perfectly functional post leg. Taper it full-length and it becomes almost a standard for use on contemporary pieces. Use it tapered but invert it so the heavy end becomes the foot and it fits in with "ranch" styling.

The cylinder can be reeded or fluted for its entire length or in limited areas, or it can taper from the center toward both ends. The latter is often done on modern pieces. The modifications can be limited or carried to the point where the original piece loses its identity completely. The same thoughts apply whether the starting shape is a cylinder, square, rectangle or what-have-you (see drawings).

Split Turnings. This generally implies a spindle which is separated on its longitudinal axis to form two identical halves. The application of the procedure in making flat-backed, half-round mouldings is easily seen but the use of the technique for forming some leg shapes is often overlooked.

The time-honored method of preparing stock for split turning is to glue two similar pieces together but with paper in the joint. This makes it possible

You can make legs on a lathe by turning variations of a cylinder . . .

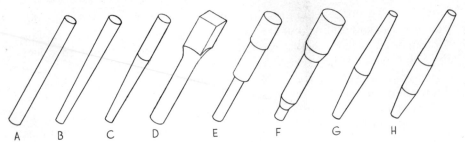

A. Straight round. B. Full taper. C. Partial taper. D. Full-round with square top which makes it easy to assemble to rails. E. Stage reduction with square shoulders. F. Stage reduction with taper transition. G. Two-way taper. H. Modified two-way taper.

Or variations of a square . . .

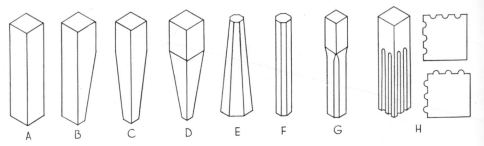

A. Straight square. B. One-side taper. C. Two-side taper. D. Four-side taper. E. Four-side taper with chamfered edges (ranch style). F. Straight with chamfered edges. G. Stopped chamfer on four edges. H. Design made with shaper or moulding head—flute and reed.

Or variations of a rectangle . . .

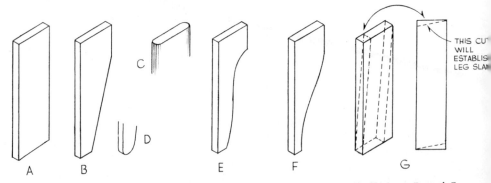

THIS CU WILL ESTABLIS LEG SLA

A. Simple rectangle. B. Tapered rectangle. C. Round foot. D. Rounded edges. E. and F. Curved inner side. G. Angled.

Or duplications of classic period styles...

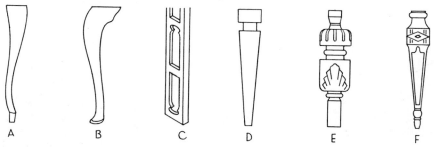

A. French Provincial. B. Queen Anne. C. Chinese Chippendale. D. Italian Provincial. E. Tudor. F. Sheraton.

to split the pieces, after turning, by using a fine, sharp chisel or knife and a mallet. Many times, however, and especially on shorter spindles, the preparations can be speeded up with other methods. One way is to hold the pieces together with screws, these being driven at the terminals where some stock and the screws can be cut off after the turning is complete. Another ideal is to use corrugated fasteners to bond the pieces. A typical split-turning procedure is shown in the drawing.

Offset Turning. The production of a lathe-turning which is oval in cross-section instead of round is a common application of offset turning. The procedure is as follows:

Each end of the spindle is marked with three centers; one being the true center, the others being the "off" centers. When you mount the stock on one off-center, it turns eccentrically so that the lathe tool is shaping one side only. When the stock is mounted on the other off-center, the opposite side is shaped and the two combined form the oval. The true center is used finally to remove the longitudinal ridge left by the initial shaping.

To predetermine the size and shape of the oval, all you have to do is make a full-size drawing of the spindle-end and then draw overlapping circles using the three centers. Once the position of the centers is established, by trial-and-error if you wish, you transfer them to the stock and begin work.

Offset turning can be used to form a clubfoot. Best bet is to make a paper pattern of the leg shape and to transfer this to two adjacent sides of the turning square. Establish a true center at each end and a single off-center at the foot end. Use a compass on a full-scale drawing of the spindle end to establish the position of the off-center. The basic shape is formed by turning the work on the true centers. This, of course, will also shape part of the foot but it will become "clubbed" when you utilize the off-center for additional turning at the foot end. As in oval-turning, a ridge will be formed but it is easily removed with sandpaper.

Cabriole Legs. The cabriole leg is certainly a style but it does not denote a particular size of leg. It can be squat and heavy, long and slender, or somewhere in between. Thus it can be used short, on a foot stool, or long, on a dining-room table.

You can produce identical legs with a split turning . . .

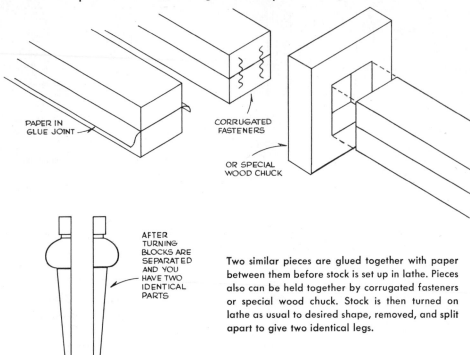

PAPER IN GLUE JOINT

CORRUGATED FASTENERS

OR SPECIAL WOOD CHUCK

AFTER TURNING BLOCKS ARE SEPARATED AND YOU HAVE TWO IDENTICAL PARTS

Two similar pieces are glued together with paper between them before stock is set up in lathe. Pieces also can be held together by corrugated fasteners or special wood chuck. Stock is then turned on lathe as usual to desired shape, removed, and split apart to give two identical legs.

Example of a leg form which is the result of the split-turning procedure. The angle of attachment was achieved by dressing the top and bottom of the leg.

Or you can cut cabriole legs without a lathe . . .

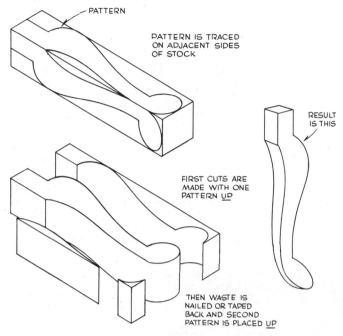

PATTERN

PATTERN IS TRACED ON ADJACENT SIDES OF STOCK

RESULT IS THIS

FIRST CUTS ARE MADE WITH ONE PATTERN UP

THEN WASTE IS NAILED OR TAPED BACK AND SECOND PATTERN IS PLACED UP

Compound cuts on a bandsaw or jigsaw can produce this shapely cabriole leg. First trace the pattern on adjacent sides of the stock, make first cuts with one side up, then replace waste material with glue or tape. Turn stock so other pattern is up and make second cuts.

It is basically a bandsaw job. The profile of the leg is drawn and then transferred to two adjacent sides of the stock. Actually it would be better to cut a cardboard template for the purpose so it can be used as often as needed. On the bandsaw, cuts are made to shape out one of the profiles. Do this to keep as much of the waste stock as possible intact. This waste is then tack-nailed or taped back in its original position, and the second profile (on the adjacent side) is cut. When the waste is removed, the cabriole shape is revealed.

After that, further modeling can be done by hand, or the piece can be lathe mounted for turning a club foot.

Blocking. Some turnings will have a square section which is smaller than the diameter of the largest turned area. While this may sometimes be achieved by stock reduction in a limited area, a more economical, and sometimes the only method that can be used, is to *add* bulk to a particular area by post blocking. This merely means that blocks are glued to a particular area to build it up to necessary size. A good wood match, a good glue job, and attention to grain direction and match are necessary for complete success. The same system, incidentally, can be used to bulk out areas on a cabriole leg so that considerably less wood is used than is the case when starting with a solid block that is large enough to do the job in itself.

YOU CAN BUY READY-MADE LEGS IN AN ASSORTMENT OF STYLES

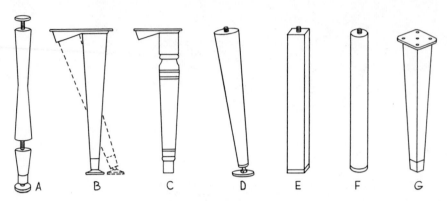

A. Combination leg, spacer and cap for two-level tables or shelves. B. Tapered legs in metal or wood with ferrule and leveler. Metal mounting plate permits vertical or slanted attachment. C. Early American style. D. Screw-top tapered leg in metal or wood. E. Square screw-topped leg. F. Round. G. Square-tapered leg in hardwood with straight mounting.

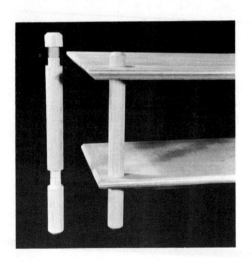

Here is how the combination leg, spacer and cap works. All you have to do is drill holes through the boards. The device makes it easy to construct either shelves or two-level tables.

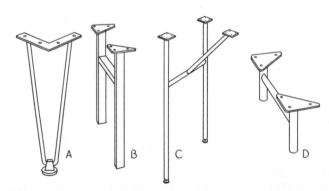

A. Hairpin wrought-iron legs obtainable in lengths from 6″ to 29″. B. H-frame wrought-iron legs. C. H-frame with strut for greater support. D. H-frame suitable for coffee tables.

LEG ANGLE CAN GIVE DESIRED STYLE TO A TABLE

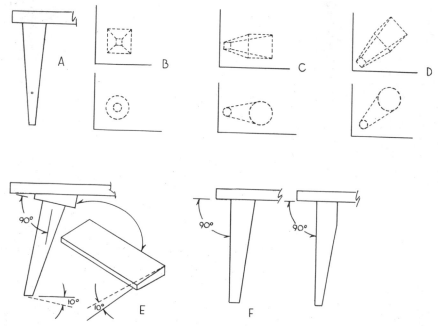

A. Side view and B, top view, of vertical leg which is cut square top and bottom. C. Slant cut on top and bottom, leg slanted in one direction. D. Slant cut top and bottom, leg slanted in two directions. E. Wedge block to give desired slant; top of leg cut square, bottom cut to match wedge. F. Impression slant gained by full or partial taper cuts on leg.

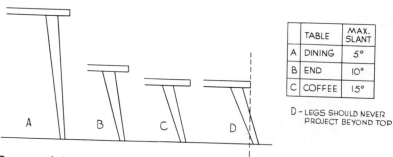

	TABLE	MAX. SLANT
A	DINING	5°
B	END	10°
C	COFFEE	15°

D – LEGS SHOULD NEVER PROJECT BEYOND TOP

Recommended angles for attaching legs to dining table, end table and coffee table.

Blocking is also a means of creating inlay effects on turnings. This is accomplished by gluing together contrasting woods to form the turning blank. Walnut and maple or birch and mahogany are examples of combinations that would produce obvious contrast.

One hint we can pass on that will make the planning of conventional turned shapes easier is to utilize the forms already available in moulding knives. Most of these have traditional shapes and when used as described in the drawing will result in professional-looking forms.

Legs may be attached directly to the underside of the furniture . . .

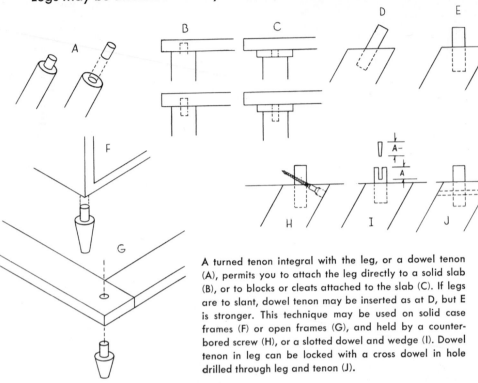

A turned tenon integral with the leg, or a dowel tenon (A), permits you to attach the leg directly to a solid slab (B), or to blocks or cleats attached to the slab (C). If legs are to slant, dowel tenon may be inserted as at D, but E is stronger. This technique may be used on solid case frames (F) or open frames (G), and held by a counterbored screw (H), or a slotted dowel and wedge (I). Dowel tenon in leg can be locked with a cross dowel in hole drilled through leg and tenon (J).

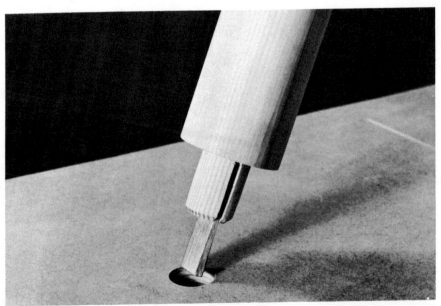

Tenon inserted in a slab can be considerably reinforced by a wedge in a slot cut in the tenon to spread the tenon tightly in the hole. Don't make the wedge too thick or you will have trouble getting tenon to "seat."

Here a wedge-locked tenon was used to attach legs to a cleat which will in turn be attached to a slab. Projecting tenon and wedge will be cut off and sanded flush. Pencil-circle indicates a lock-dowel which passes through the leg and the dowel that forms the tenon.

Or legs may be attached to rails which are attached to top . . .

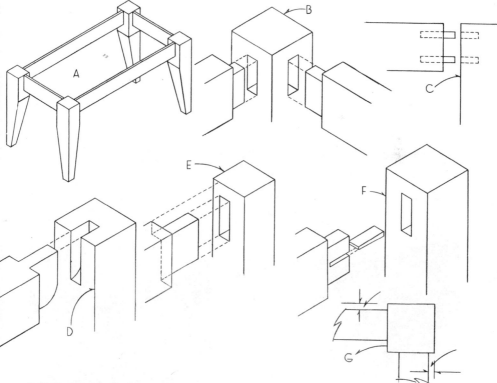

A. Typical leg-and-rail assembly. B. Mortise-tenon joint for attaching legs to rail is strong but should be made on a drill press for best results. C. Dowel joint is easier to make, accomplishes the same thing. D. Stub tenon is easily done with dado on table saw. Note how tenon is shaped to conform with arc left by dado. E. One-sided tenon is useful when rail is of thin material. F. Slotted tenon is locked by wedge for extra strength. G. When rails are inset slightly, joint is less noticeable than if they were flush with legs.

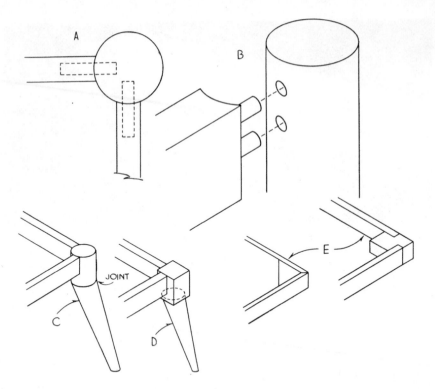

Round legs can be used in leg-and-rail assembly if end of rail is shaped on drum sander to conform to leg (A and B). Two-piece leg (C and D) can have either a round or a square top. Corner blocks (E) provide a seat for attaching the leg, thus eliminating the rail-to-leg joint.

Here is a combination dowel-and-tenon joint that provides a locking device which will keep parts together even if the glue fails. The dowels on the one rail pass through half the leg and enter the holes drilled in the tenon on the other rail.

This is an original leg-and-rail joint which is not difficult to make. It has great strength plus a locking feature. The rails are notched for a cross-lap joint and fit into cross-slots formed in the leg.

READY-MADE LEGS. Among the many areas in which the modern home-craftsman is fortunate is the realm of the "ready-mades"—those furniture components which are all shaped and sanded and ready for assembly to a project. If you don't already know, you'll be happy to discover that there is an impressive assortment of ready-made legs, with good variety in style, size, and materials, available today; many of them at less cost than you would have to pay for the raw material with which to make them. The saving in time is also significant. And, maybe most gratifying, is the fact that lack of equipment need not be as limiting as you might think. Here are typical examples:

Need early American legs but lack a lathe? You can buy them ready-made in sizes that go from 4″ up to 28″. Don't let lack of a bandsaw stop you from thinking about French Provincial legs for these are also available ready-made in sizes that will do for many projects. A glance through the two catalogs mentioned early in this book reveal that many other styles are available—Empire, Queen Anne (plain or carved), Provincial, even legs with a carved ball-claw. There is a considerable assortment of square-tapered and round-tapered legs both in wood and metal and many types of wrought-iron legs in both stationary and folding designs.

The point is—don't let the fabrication of legs throw you. It seems to be a critical point for many people and, after reading the above, you'll agree that it should not be so.

One thing though, don't make the project and then buy the legs to tack on almost like an afterthought. Have them on hand when you do the initial planning.

ATTACHING LEGS. Since legs must forever bear the weight of the project, plus, in some cases, the weight of people, and in other cases the weight of items stored in or on the project, leg direction and methods of attachment should get special consideration. The durability of some projects such as tables and chairs is directly attributable to the strength of the leg attachment-joint. When the project comes apart it is usually at the point where the legs join the rest of the assembly.

Appearance, of course, must also be considered and this will, occasionally, justify a compromise but not to the point where you must tolerate a weak joint. In such cases you can design the joint for appearance but include reinforcement for strength. Such reinforcement can take the form of concealed glue-blocks, dowel-locks, screws, nails, or even nuts and bolts.

The leg-and-rail assembly, with mortise-tenon or dowel joints used to join

Legs for two-level tables require middle-joints . . .

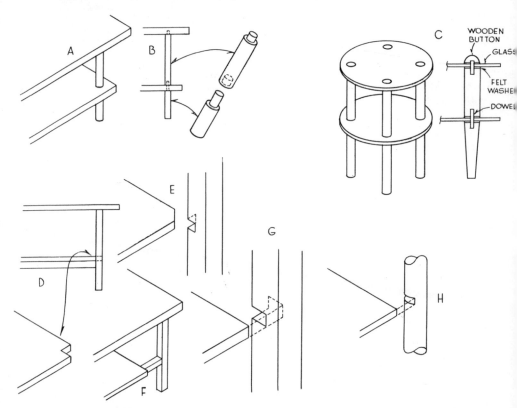

A. Middle shelf on a table is practical and adds strength. B. With round legs, simple dowel joint through shelf works well. C. For glass-topped tables, dowel joint and felt "washers" are used. D. With square legs, rest shelf on stretchers and notch it to fit around leg. E. Without stretcher, leg can be notched this way or as at G. At F, shelf extends only part way and rests on stretcher. H. Notching technique also works with round legs.

pieces, is generally considered one of the more satisfactory methods of constructing a strong under-structure. When legs are short, rails alone are sufficient; when legs are long, and particularly when slant is involved, stretchers are added to keep legs from pulling apart.

The leg-rail construction is found not only on different styles but on different pieces. It is not, as a quick thought might indicate, confined to tables. A chest of drawers can have leg-and-rail underpinnings and so can a cabinet or a desk. A chair is basically leg-and-rail construction; it's just that the back legs extend above the level of the rails to form the back of the chair. A stool or bench can be simply leg-and-rail under-structure to support a padded slab.

One hint passed on by professional cabinetmakers is, when possible, to avoid a flush joint where the rail meets the leg. It's best to set the rail back (⅛″ is okay) so that a hair-line crack which could eventually develop at that point due to shrinkage of the parts won't be as obvious as it might if the parts were flush.

But the leg-and-rail technique is not the only way to attach legs nor is it always possible to use it. For reasons of style or design it may be necessary to attach legs separately directly to a slab, and there are ways to do this which provide maximum strength. Legs may be cut directly in a slab which is used as the end member of a case, or the legs may be the bottom terminal of posts which form the corners of a project.

Best bet is to study the ideas shown here in drawings and photos and to adapt them or use them as is to suit your own needs. As we get further into the book we will be discussing leg attachment as it applies to specific pieces.

CHAPTER THIRTEEN

RAILS AND FRAMES

RAILS. In actual practice, a rail is a bar of wood (or other material) which joins two other pieces. We've already discussed the assembly called "leg-and-rail" and have seen that it is a fairly basic piece of design which is applicable, in one form or another, to many projects. The peripheral pieces on a paneled slab might also be called rails although the four pieces, as a whole, would be a frame. There are times when a rail is not a rail but an "apron" even

RAILS FORM THE DIVIDING ELEMENTS THAT SUPPORT DRAWERS

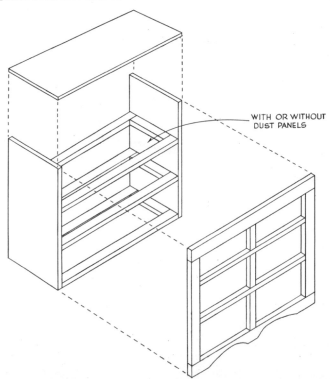

WITH OR WITHOUT
DUST PANELS

though its shape, method of joining, and its purpose remain fairly consistent. An apron (sometimes called a skirt) is a horizontal bar of wood which extends between the tops of legs or feet. Examples are the bottom of a chair seat, the underside of a table, the bottom of a chest, etc. The distinction between rail and apron (or skirt) seems to be whether the part is placed high enough (in the case of legs) to touch the slab under which it is placed. It seems to have become an arbitrary decision or maybe just a case of semantics, but be that as it may and call the horizontal bar one or the other, the important consideration as far as construction is concerned is that these are basically "strength" pieces. They are major factors in the durability of a project and therefore must join other pieces in a manner that will provide maximum strength.

It's not the purpose of this section to establish identity but to demonstrate assemblies and joints with such pieces so the techniques will be applicable on all projects.

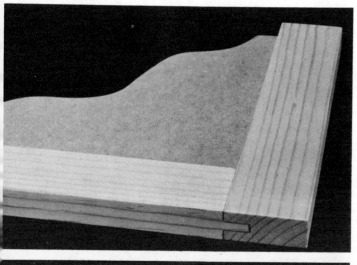

Typical construction of rails and inserted dust panel, which is quite practical for use as the horizontal frame between drawers in a chest. Joints are easily accomplished with a dado head or even a regular saw blade.

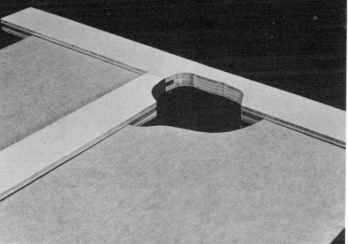

Typical middle-joint when a center rail is used to provide additional strength and rigidity on a long frame. The end of the rail is "tongued" to fit the same groove formed for the dust panel.

Examples of other end-joints that can be used on rails. A. This joint, which has already been seen, is simply a groove running along the inside edges of the side rails into which the tongues cut in the end rails fit. B. Half-lap joint. C. Notched rail. D. Simple butt joint.

Even simple joints can be easily reinforced for strength. Here a notched joint is strengthened with a dowel which is in turn locked with a nail. On thin stock it is a good idea to drill lead holes for the nails.

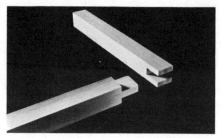

A tenon joint is easy to make with either dado head or saw blade. Make the tenon one-third the thickness of the stock.

The dowel joint is always reliable. Two dowels are always better than one; they prevent the piece from twisting.

Methods of attaching rail-assemblies to the sides of a case . . .

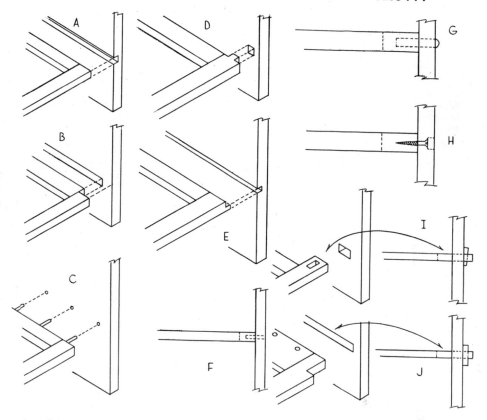

A. Full-length dado is easy to make, but cut can be seen from front unless covered with moulding frame. B. Stopped dado leaves no exposed cuts. C. Dowel joint. Best way to locate dowel holes in panel is to drive small brads in dowel locations on rails, snip off heads, and press rail against panel so brads mark drilling points. D. Mortise and tenon. E. Rabbet and dado. F. Dowel joint with dowels going through panel, sanded flush on outside. G. Dowels left raised for decorative effect. H. Butt joint held with screws hidden by dowel plugs. I. Wedge-locked tenon for unusual style. J. Similar joint but with dowels used instead of wedges.

FRAMES. In this category of "frames" we include the skeleton frame, which is basically a system of rails on which to hang a cover material; and the solid frame, which is typified by the assembly of top, bottom, and side slabs in a case.

Skeleton Frame. This type of frame can be used on free-standing pieces although its use doesn't seem to make much sense when plywood and similar slab materials are so widely available and in such variety. In this regard the frame provides the strength and so serves to permit the use of thin materials too weak to stand alone or too fine for conventional joinery. When a particularly intriguing, but thin, slab material is available, the choice of a skeleton frame may be one of necessity. It *can* be economical since the frame pieces will be covered, thus permitting the use of cheap, although sound, material; and thin slabs (used as the cover material) are cheaper than thick slabs.

THIN SLABS OVER A SKELETON FRAME FORM A CASE

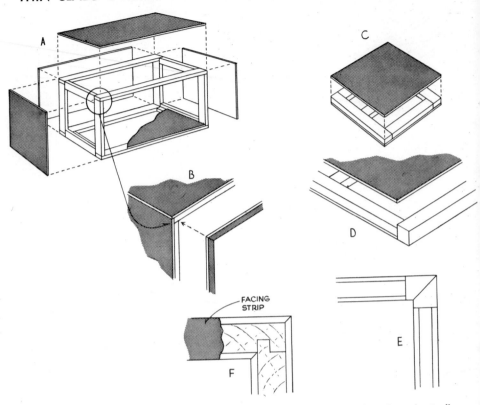

FACING STRIP

A. Example of skeleton frame for a case. Covering material is glued and mechanically fastened. B. Front edges may be banded with similar material. C. Panels may be attached to skeleton frames and then used as solid slabs. D. Another technique is to allow exposed, solid-wood edges which can then be shaped for joining, as at E. F. Open skeleton frame can be assembled with fancier joints than those shown at A and then covered.

Joints used in constructing a skeleton frame must be just as strong as those used elsewhere, even though appearance is not as important. This joins parts going in three directions.

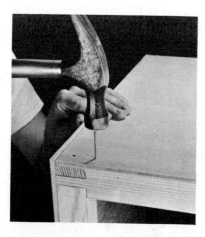

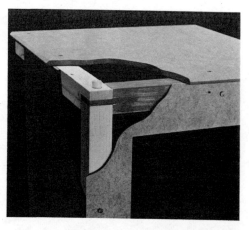

Cover material can be applied with nails or with glue or contact cement when appearance is paramount. Front edges would be banded with same material to conceal joints and grain.

Here is the same joint, but the addition of a lock-dowel makes it impossible for the pieces to separate. Drill the hole for the dowel while parts are held in correct position—by nailing if necessary.

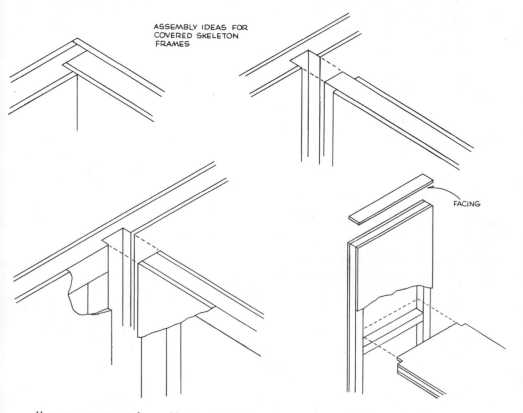

ASSEMBLY IDEAS FOR COVERED SKELETON FRAMES

FACING

Here are some ways of assembling covered skeleton frames to form a case. The cover material can be cut longer than the frame in certain places to cover the joints (top left and lower right). At upper right, cover material is cut short of frame edge to allow only the frame to fit in the dado.

Skeleton frame can be used to construct a built-in which will cover the entire wall of a room. Note that some of the frame members are utilized as supports for shelves. Installing a face-frame and then hanging the doors will complete the project.

PLYWOOD OR GLUED-UP STOCK ALSO FORMS A FRAME

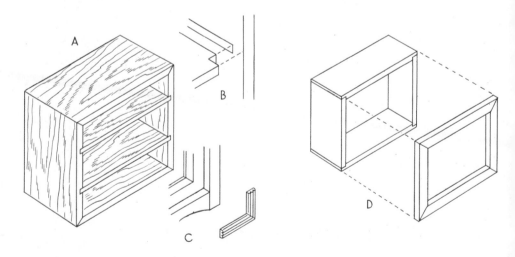

A. Frame of slabs can be joined at edges in many ways; dividers or shelves can be let into the sides in dadoes. B. Blind dadoes avoid cut at front of case. C. Front edges may be banded, decoratively framed, or hidden with moulding. D. Front frame is the means of hanging hinged doors, or it may be grooved for sliding doors.

It is not a means of doing a job faster; it certainly isn't a procedure that permits less careful craftsmanship even though it might let you get away with less attention to details and with easier-to-do joints since nails, screws, glue-blocks, and corrugated fasteners could be used and then hidden. But the frame would have to be as strong as any furniture carcass.

The skeleton frame is more applicable in built-ins where an existing floor, wall, or ceiling is utilized as a component of the project.

Solid Frame. The assembly of slabs which requires no support other than the joints which bond the parts together and which may be further strengthened by the addition of other components such as shelves, dividers, stiles, etc., is a more practical and more acceptable method of forming the frame which is the basic form for all case-goods. In picturing a frame, in this section, as being those pieces which comprise the top, bottom and sides or ends of a case, we need consider only those two areas where these parts are joined: where the bottom connects to the sides; where the top connects to the sides.

When the frame corners are flush, joint considerations are pretty much the same although the top joints often receive more attention than the bottom ones. Different methods are used when the top slab projects beyond the sides and front. Quite often in this situation, the strength and rigidity of the frame is in the joints which connect sides to bottom and midway components to sides. Thus, if the top is put in place merely with a few screws to keep it in position, the frame as a whole will still have sufficient strength.

The simple butt joint is used quite often, even on commercial pieces. The secret of achieving a professional appearance is to sand the exposed end sufficiently to give it a slick look. Cutting a shallow kerf just below the edge also helps to enhance the joint.

When the top projects beyond the sides and front of a case, you can make every joint with dowels and produce a piece that is strong and professional looking.

A combination of dado and rabbet results in a joint that locks itself. This is an effective joint to use on a frame bottom when legs are going to be attached.

CHAPTER FOURTEEN

DRAWERS

THE EXPERT furniture buyer considers good drawer construction a mark of quality. The practical reason for this is that drawers take a beating and must hold together for a long time. The theoretical reason is that the maker can save considerable time, money, and material by skimping on drawer construction and therefore the degree of quality here is a good indication of the quality of the piece as a whole. Well, whether you go along with the theory or merely consider the practical reasons, you should agree that drawers ought to be well made no matter what the eventual contents.

The basic form of a drawer is a box without a top. If all you had to consider was strength, then it's conceivable that thick lumber, mated with butt joints and reinforced with glue, nails, screws, and glue-blocks, would be successful. If you were going to store cotton balls and appearance was not a factor, you could get along with an apple crate, or you could store handkerchiefs in a cigar box. There really are times when these examples could be used quite nicely, if the location and the project and the storage items permit it; but in furniture, refinements, made necessary by practical and esthetic considerations, are definitely in order.

Stress in a drawer is mostly down on the drawer bottom because of the drawer contents and at the points where the drawer front is joined to the sides. When you open a drawer you are, in effect, attempting to pull off the drawer front. To avoid this, the front-to-sides joints should be strong and should, preferably, lock. That's why quality furniture buyers look for the dovetail at these points. A discriminating buyer might even be disappointed if the drawer *back* was not dovetailed.

The dovetail is an excellent example of a joint which will hold together even when the glue fails. But it is not the only joint with such characteristics. Actually, it should not be the paramount factor in judging over-all furniture quality since modern machinery will turn out dovetails like a machine extruding spaghetti. You will find dovetails even on cheap furniture.

It is not our purpose to belittle the dovetail—far from it. It is our intention

A DRAWER IS BASICALLY AN OPEN BOX

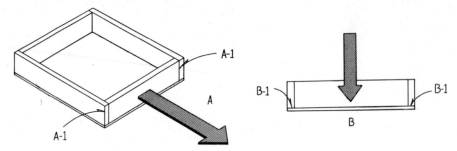

Aside from appearance, there are two important reasons why a drawer is not as simple to construct as the box above. Pulling out a drawer (A), creates strain at points A-1; and loading a drawer (B) creates strain at points B-1. Use strong joints at these places.

Drawer front should be strong, in harmony with rest of piece . . .

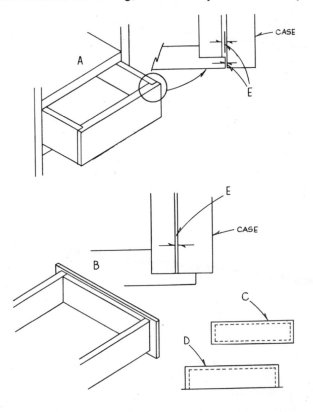

Front can be flush with the case edges (A) or overlap edges (B). By using a second piece, front can overlap on four edges (C) or on three (D). Provide clearance of 1/16″ (E) so drawer will work smoothly.

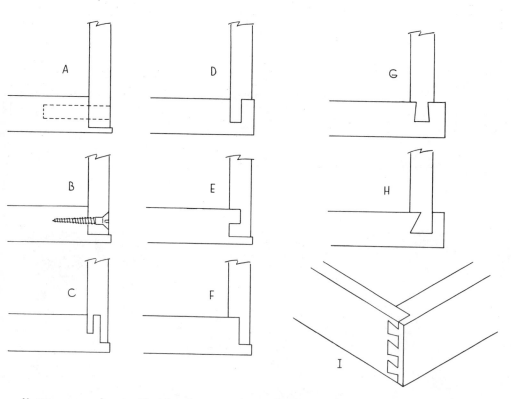

Here are some front-to-side joints for constructing drawers: A. Pegged joint with dowels. B. Simple rabbet reinforced with nails or screws. C. Combination groove and rabbet joint. D. Rabbet and dado joint. E. Another type of rabbet and dado joint. F. Side rabbeted joint. G. Dovetail and dovetail slot. H. Half-dovetail. I. Dovetail—exposed or blind.

Unique design for drawer fronts conceals the case edges and gives the whole piece a trim appearance. Fronts are cut on a 45-degree miter and fit into matching cut in case edges.

Methods of attaching drawer back . . .

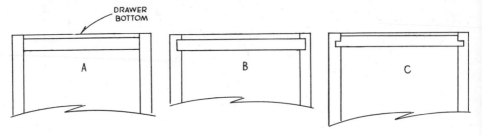

DRAWER
BOTTOM

A B C

A. Simple butt joint. B. Dado. C. Dado and rabbet.

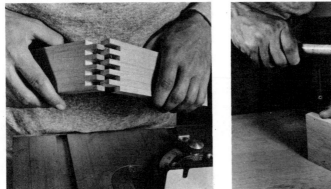

Finger-lap joint (left) is sometimes used on drawer backs, provides lots of gluing area. Joint can be locked with a dowel tapped into a hole drilled not greater than half the thickness of the stock (right).

to ease your mind so you won't feel guilty or inadequate when drawer projects lack the dovetail. But you should be aware of the *features* of the dovetail and attempt to incorporate similar characteristics in other joints which are easier to do. Before we leave the dovetail, remember that there are commercial jigs on the market which can be used on a drill press or with a portable router to turn out dovetails slick and quick.

The pegged drawer front, which we demonstrate here in photos and drawings, is a good substitute for the dovetail and certainly easier to do. Other joints with similar characteristics are also shown. The drawer front should harmonize with the style of the piece and generally should be of ¾″ stock. This is substantial enough for rigidity and thick enough so you won't have trouble making joints.

The drawer sides can be thinner—⅝″ or ½″ stock—but here too the material used should be strong. Relieve or at least round off the top edges of the side pieces. The drawer bottom should be let in to the drawer sides and also the front. Thickness of the bottom piece depends on the size of the drawer and what you will store in it, but ⅛″ is about a minimum. A ¼″ thickness is better;

Methods of attaching drawer bottom . . .

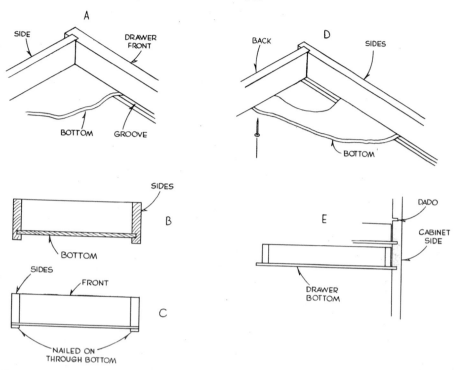

Bottom can be of hardboard, between ⅛″ and ½″ thick, and let into grooves in the front and sides (A and B). Drawer back is cut narrower than the sides, and bottom is nailed to its edge (D). If only hand tools are available, strips can be nailed through bottom into sides (C). Extended bottoms (E) provide slides to fit in dadoes in cabinet sides—a good idea for small shop drawers.

if necessary, you can go as high as ¼″. Hardboard is a good material for drawer bottoms because it is stiff, smooth and doesn't warp.

The thickness of the drawer back can match the drawer sides. It should, preferably, be let in to dado cuts formed in the side pieces.

All inside and outside surfaces of drawer parts should be carefully sanded and, at least, sealed. Surfaces should feel smooth to the touch; all edges should be slightly rounded by working them with sandpaper.

INSTALLING DRAWERS. Installation of a drawer means the method used to guide it smoothly in and out of the opening. There are many ways to do this, and the methods range from the use of ready-made hardware with wheels and rollers to no guides at all—simply a box sliding in a box. The *classic* method, and one which you will find on most quality furniture, employs a guide which is attached to the case or frame, and a runner or slide which is attached to the drawer.

The guide is a straight, smooth bar of wood firmly attached at each end and carefully positioned so the drawer will not rub against the sides of the

HOW TO INSTALL DRAWERS IN A CHEST

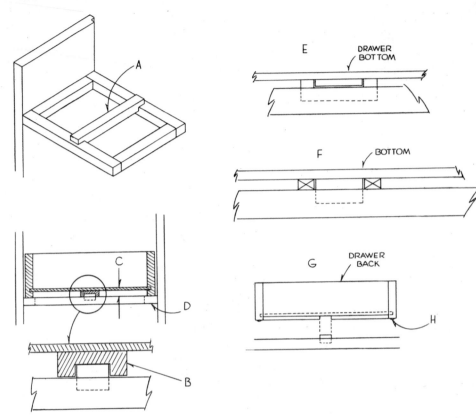

Guide bar (A) is rabbet cut at ends to fit over front and back rails. U-shaped runner (B) is attached to drawer bottom with nails or screws at front and back. Thickness of guide and runner must be such that drawer rests on its sides (D). To minimize dimension C, you can use a channel as the guide and a plain strip of wood as the runner (E), or use two strips as a guide (F). You can also notch the drawer back (G) and let it act as the runner. Thumb tacks (H) help drawer to slide smoothly.

Typical drawer guide rabbeted at ends to fit over front and rear rails in a cabinet (left). The slide is glued to the drawer bottom and reinforced with fasteners driven into the front and back (right). Note use of glue blocks.

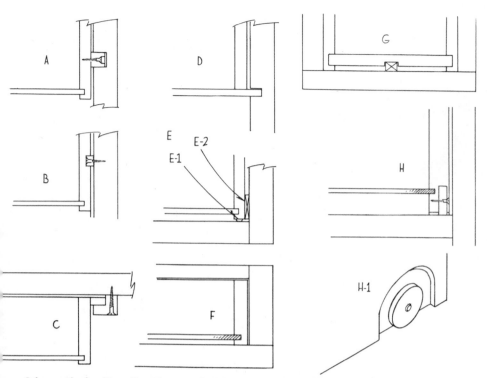

Other methods of installing drawers: A. Runner screwed to drawer side rides in dado cut in case side. B. Reverse of A; dado cut in drawer rides on runner screwed to case. C. Drawer hung on rabbeted strip, runner attached to drawer sides. D. Extended drawer bottom rides in dadoes cut in case sides. E. Drawer rides on dome glides (E-1), guided by strip (E-2) attached to drawer side. F. Drawer rides on its own sides—no guides or runners. G. Extra-heavy drawer bottom with groove to ride on center guide. H. Drawer rides on thin wheels of hardwood, metal or plastic installed in recess cut in drawer sides (H-1).

These darkroom drawers were built with extended bottoms which ride in dadoes formed in the case sides. This is a practical method when appearance is not important.

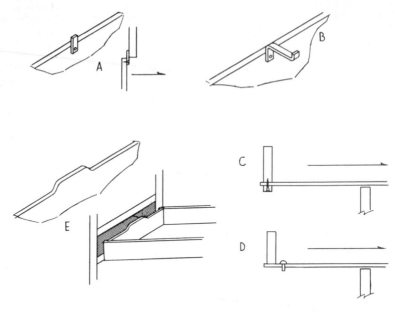

A. Hardwood block or metal strip screwed to drawer back hits front frame when drawer is pulled out too far. B. Bent-up metal strip. C. Wood block screwed to underside of drawer hits frame. D. Rivet pressed through hole drilled in drawer bottom. E. Shaped drawer back, tilt drawer when inserting.

case. The slide is a similar piece of wood, broader than, and grooved to fit over, the guide. These pieces do not require bulk; their purpose is to guide, not carry, the weight of the drawer. In the most common application, the guide is rabbeted at each end and attached to the front and rear rails of the frame with a touch of glue and a few nails, or maybe a single screw at each end. The slide is glued to the drawer bottom with possibly a nail angle-driven into the drawer front and another into the drawer back. You can dispense with the glue if you attach the slide firmly to the front and rear drawer components. When the drawer back extends below the drawer bottom, the back must be notched so the slide can be fitted.

When the case has no horizontal frames, this system of course can't be used since there is no place to attach the guide. Then guides and runners must be attached to the sides of the drawer and to the inner surfaces of the case. Common method is to attach cleats (guides) to the case sides and to groove the drawer sides. Thus you have a guide-and-slide arrangement, but in this situation the entire weight of the drawer and its contents is on the cleat, with the drawer side also coming in for its share of the stress. This could be reversed by putting the cleat on the drawer side and forming the grooves in the case side. One basis for making the choice is whether the drawer fronts will be flush with the case edges or whether they will lip over. When they are flush, it's better to attach the guide cleats to the case and groove the drawer sides. When the drawer front has a lip which will conceal the case edges you can use the alternate method.

When the design puts the stress on the guide-and-slide, then the ultimate use of the drawer is an important factor in determining the size of the cleat used as the guide. For example, a ¼" square piece of pine may do nicely as the guide for a drawer in which you will store handkerchiefs, but certainly not for a shop drawer that will hold heavy tools. The sketches in this section will show other methods as well as some variations of the more commonly used techniques.

STORAGE. Drawers can be great space-wasters. So many times a deep drawer is designed and used to store shallow items with the result that 50 percent of the precious cubic inches are thrown away. Check through existing drawers and chances are that only the lower halves are being utilized.

You can make your own decorative drawer pulls . . .

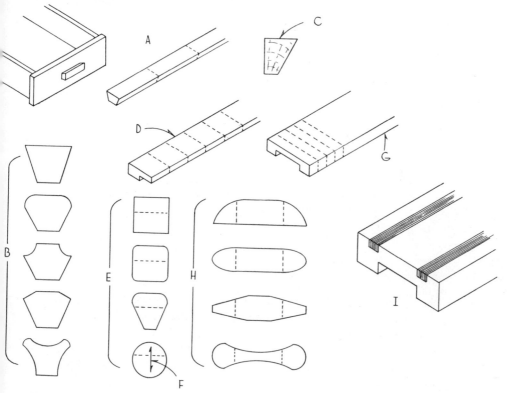

The basic piece may be a strip, bevel-cut on opposite edges (A), which is cut into segments and left as is, or shaped into one of the forms shown at B. Or the strip may be beveled on only one side (C). The strip may be rabbet cut (D) and shaped into any of the forms at E, making sure grain runs in direction shown at F, for greatest strength. The basic strip may have a wide groove (G) and be shaped as at H. The strip may even be inlayed with a contrasting wood before cutting (I).

Or you can make drawers with built-in pulls . . .

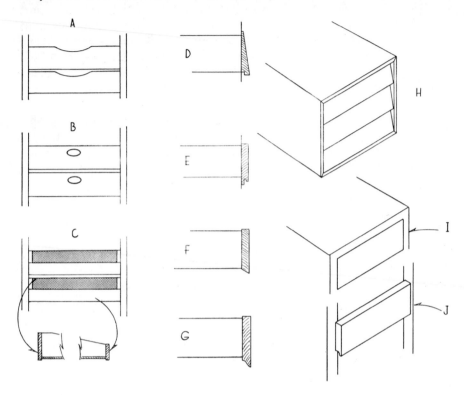

Shape the top of the drawer (A) to leave space for fingers, or form an opening in the front (B). In bin-type drawers (C), the front is lower than the back, allowing room for fingers. Bottom edge of drawer front can be shaped for the fingers (D thru G). Drawers may be set within the framework of the case (H), may be flush with case (I), or may overlap (J).

The secret lies in planning the interior of the drawer for the particular items it will hold. This will not only lead to greater space utilization but also to greater protection for the contents. Kitchen-cabinet drawers, for example, when used to store flatware, don't have to be more than 2″ or 3″ deep. But they are usually closer to 6″ deep. Result is that you waste the space in the upper half unless you pile item on item. A simple way to utilize *all* the space is to install a sliding tray to create another level for more storage. This doesn't have to be more than a small slab which rests on cleats nailed to the inside of the drawer sides. So you can get to all the items on the lower level (the drawer bottom), the tray should not be wider than half the drawer length.

The tray can be partitioned or fitted with special racks; it can be used as a tote tray. A housewife, for example, can use such a tray to carry flatware to the table or from the sink to the drawer. Thus you add convenience as well as storage space.

Egg-crate dividers are very efficient in many areas, from storing small parts in the shop to socks in the bedroom. Wells can be made by boring large holes; troughs by making cove cuts. Dowels can be used as spindles to store items with a center hole, such as spools of thread.

Don't waste space; don't make it inconvenient to use the project. Consider the depth of the drawer in relation to ultimate use, and consider the interior in terms of particular storage items.

PLAN INTERIOR OF A DRAWER FOR BEST USE OF SPACE

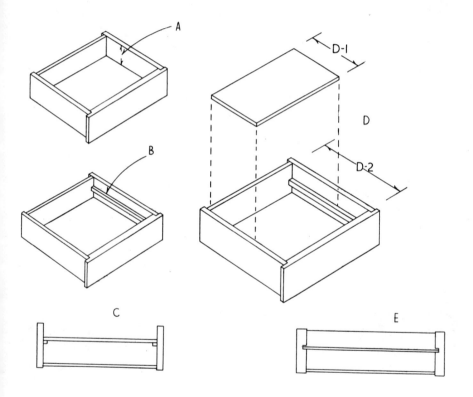

A. Full capacity of a drawer is seldom utilized, especially when flat items are stored. B. Easy way to gain space is to use cleats on which a sliding tray can ride (C). D. The tray should not interfere with getting things from any part of the drawer; thus D-1 should never be more than half of D-2. The sliding shelf may ride in dadoes cut in drawer sides (E), but this prevents removing the shelf.

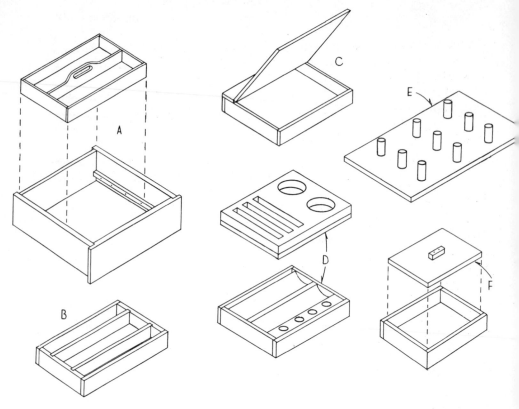

The sliding shelf (above) can be made in the form of a lift-out tote tray with a handle (A) or without (B). It can be a box with a hinged cover (C), or it can be compartmentalized for special items (D). Pegs can be fitted in the tray for storing spools of thread (E), or a fitted cover can be made for holding down papers (F).

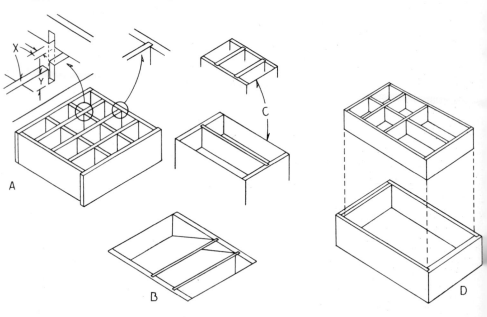

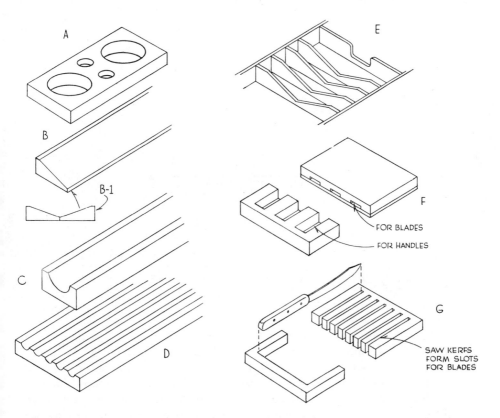

Some more drawer-storage ideas: A. Holes cut through board with fly-cutter or router provide wells for paper clips, tacks, etc. B. Bevel-cut strip attached to matching strip (B-1) provides a trough. D. Cove cuts on table saw make pencil trays. E. Divisions for kitchen flatware. F. and G. Two ideas for storing knives.

Drawer can be divided to hold small items (opposite page). A. Eggcrate division: X equals thickness of stock; Y equals half the stock width. B. Slanted divisions for paper storage. C. Simple divisions can be set in dadoes. D. Divisions for existing drawers can be made as a separate assembly.

CHAPTER FIFTEEN

DOORS

A DOOR doesn't add structural strength to a project but it can add, or detract, from its appearance and it can make the project more, or less, convenient to use. The door, if it is a fabricated component, must be a strong assembly in itself, and the method used to install it must be firm and durable.

Most doors are slabs—framed or unframed—but they can be many other things. Slim slats can be assembled in a vertical pattern to make tambour doors that will turn corners. Sections can be hinged so they will fold back on themselves. Horizontal slats can be inserted in frames to make louvered doors, or you can combine louvers with slabs. Decorator effects or particular style treatments are achieved by the shape of frame pieces when inserted slabs are used or when mouldings are used to create a pattern on a slab. Pierced effects are possible on solid slabs or by assembling pre-cut, narrow pieces; you can even "weave" a door by using thin and narrow strips of wood.

Doors can swing on hinges, slide in grooves, fold back on themselves, even disappear. And sometimes, as in the case of drop doors, they may also serve as a writing or serving surface. Doors on most furniture pieces either swing or slide.

HINGED DOORS. Hinged doors give maximum accessibility to contents but they require room in which to swing them open. Sliding doors do not require "swing" room but they reduce accessibility by 50 percent. When the normal swing for hinged doors is a problem and sliding doors just won't do, you can consider using hinges at the top or the bottom of the door. In such a case the door could be opened wide even if the project was hemmed in on both sides by adjacent walls or other furniture.

Hinges may be used on framed or unframed door slabs and the door itself may be set in flush with the case edges, or butted against the case edges; or it could be a combination of both such as the "cabinet-door lip," which is basically a rabbet cut.

Most any slab material can be used to make a door. Thin, ready-made slab materials are ideal for sliding doors and for framed, panel doors. These materials include plywood, hardboards (plain, perforated, or pierced), particleboard, laminates, etc. You can make a thick door and do it economically by covering both sides of a frame with one of the above-mentioned materials —a hollow-core construction. At times, it's possible to get away with covering just one side. A perforated hardboard can be very functional when used on the back of a door since, when used with clips and hooks made for the purpose, it provides ready-to-use storage facilities. Most of the ideas and techniques described for forming framed slabs can be used to make doors.

Solid-lumber doors are formed in the manner described for making solid-lumber slabs. Be especially careful about making them from many narrow pieces rather than a few wide ones since doors must be self-sufficient and all construction must serve to prevent warpage. Solid-lumber doors may also be formed by assembling boards vertically with horizontal cleats (or battens) across the back to secure them. The door boards do not have to be edge-glued but the mating edges should be matched to minimize (visually) any separation that might occur. The matching can be done with a tongue-and-groove or with rabbet cuts or with any of the joints described in a previous section. On utility jobs where you don't wish to bother with either edge-gluing or matching, you can achieve a similar result by chamfering the top corners of the mating edges.

We might mention a kind of slab-on-slab idea which makes it possible to achieve a rabbeted edge (cabinet-door lip) without having to shape it with saw blade, shaper, or router. Basically, the idea is this: Cut one slab to fit *inside* the door opening. Then cut a second slab of thinner material that overlaps the case edges. Bonding the second slab to the first one gives you a door, in effect, with a rabbeted edge. Instead of a base slab, you could use an open frame. An open frame could also be covered on both sides—the back cover to match the frame dimensions, the front to extend and so form the rabbet.

HINGES AND THEIR INSTALLATION. There are many types and styles of hinges—some of them good for general use, others with particular characteristics which make them most applicable for special purposes. To attempt a history would result in unnecessary detailing, many facets of which would be outside the scope of furniture making. It's best to make the obvious point that a hinge is a piece of hardware that supplies a pivot action on which a door can swing to open or close. The truth is that you can hang just about any door by not going much further than the simple butt hinge.

There are a few other basic considerations, the most important of which applies generally: the hinge must bear the weight of the door plus whatever else is on the door, and it must do this through countless openings and closings. If a lead hole for screws is needed, keep it as small as possible so the screws will grip with maximum strength. Two hinges will usually do the job, but if the door is unusually heavy or large, then install a third hinge at the center. A 1″ butt hinge will do for most furniture projects since doors are

HOW TO INSTALL HINGED DOORS

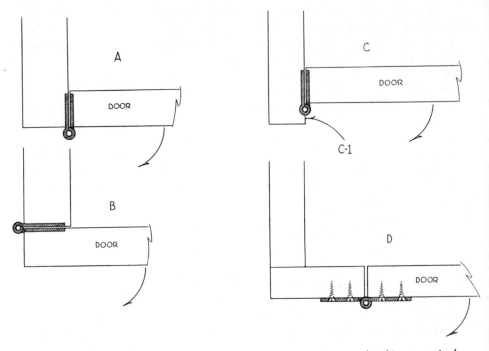

Four basic ways to hang doors with butt hinges: A. Door flush with case edge, hinges mortised. B. Door overlapping case edge, hinges mortised. C. Door inset beyond case edge, hinges mortised, C-1 is natural stop. D. Door flush with case edge, hinges surface-mounted.

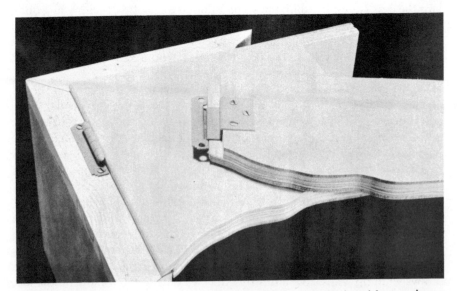

Semiconcealed offset hinges are used on lipped doors, shown here back and front to demonstrate proper method of installation. Door may be lipped by cutting a rabbet around its edge, or by attaching a thin panel of slightly larger dimensions.

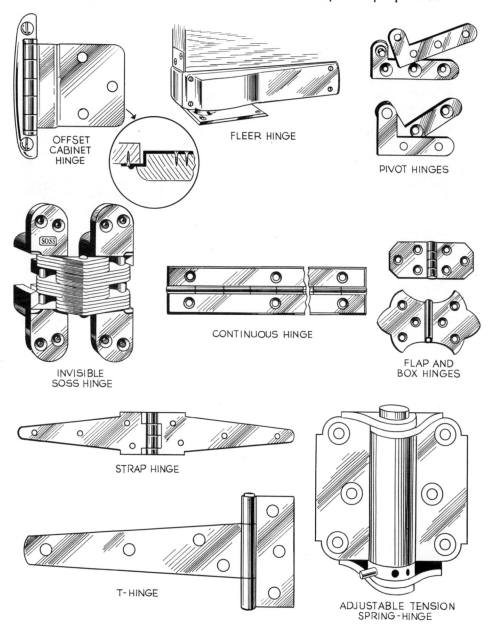

OFFSET CABINET HINGE

FLEER HINGE

PIVOT HINGES

INVISIBLE SOSS HINGE

CONTINUOUS HINGE

FLAP AND BOX HINGES

STRAP HINGE

T-HINGE

ADJUSTABLE TENSION SPRING-HINGE

seldom more than 2′ wide. Consider a 2″ butt hinge for doors over this. Closet doors, room doors, and doors on large built-ins may require a 3″ hinge.

Butt Hinges. Hinges may be concealed, semiconcealed, or surface-mounted. Often, hinges together with other matching hardware are used as decorative details. The butt hinge is usually installed so the pin loops are visible from the front. This means, when a door is inset, that one leaf of the hinge is attached to the case side (or the frontal frame), the other to the door edge.

Invisible Soss hinges fit into holes drilled in edge of door and side of case, as shown in this cutaway photo (left). Hinges allow door to open completely (right) but are invisible when door is closed.

Single doors must be stopped at case edge . . .

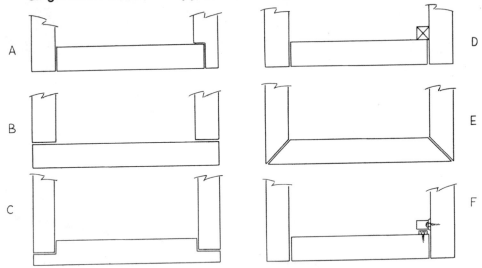

A. Door flush with case can be stopped by rabbeting case edge. B. Overlapping door stopped by case edge. C. Door rabbeted on four sides. D. Wooden or metal cleat used as a stop. E. Mitered door edge stopped by matching cut in case edge. F. Magnetic catch both stops door and holds it closed.

In order to reduce the gap between door edge and case side, both components are mortised. The length of the mortise (or the "gain" as it is sometimes called) should be as long as the hinge. The width of the mortise should equal the width of one hinge-leaf but only to the base of the pin loops. The depth of the mortise should equal the thickness of the hinge-leaf—no more, no less.

Best bet for accurate installation is to put the door in the opening (holding it with slim wedges if necessary) and to mark both door and case for hinge location. Then remove the door and use the hinge itself as a template to mark the mortise areas. *Be especially careful about depth.* The mortise may be cleaned out quickly if you have a portable router. Otherwise use a sharp knife to outline the cut and a chisel to remove the waste. If you do get into trouble with the mortise depth, you can compensate (if too deep) by using paper or thin cardboard under the hinge. Take your time when installing hinges, no matter what kind. Messy workmanship here can interfere with smooth operation of the door, may make repair work necessary, and may detract from the appearance of the entire project.

Offset Hinges. These are used to hang lipped doors. The important consideration is that the rabbet cut in the door should match the amount of offset in the hinge. A common error is to arbitrarily cut the rabbet and then try to find a hinge to suit. While offset hinges are made in different sizes, they

Double doors present another problem . . .

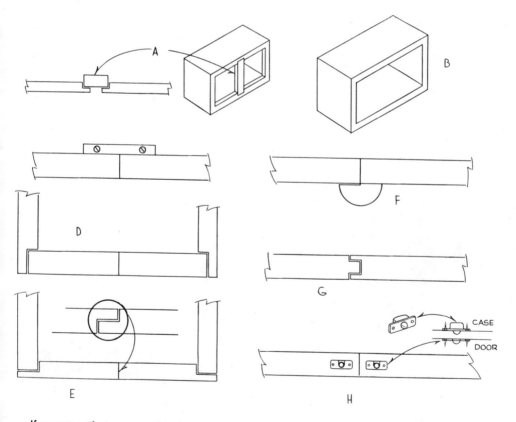

If a center-stile is present (A), then it serves same function as case edge. But if there is no stile (B), door can be stopped by: C. Cleat screwed to top or bottom of case. D. Rabbeted case edge. E. Rabbeted door edge. F. Wooden moulding. G. Tongue and groove in door edges. H. Bullet catch.

are not available to match *every* situation. Have the hinges on hand before you cut. Offset hinges are available in many styles for either surface-mounting or semiconcealment.

Other types of hinges are shown in the drawings and some of the photos will show the installation of the Soss hinge, which is truly an invisible hinge and quite simple to use.

SLIDING DOORS. Sliding doors are very popular on contemporary pieces and easy to make and install whether you work with hand or power tools. Major objection is that they cut down on accessibility of the project's contents by 50 percent, but this is important only if 100 percent accessibility is necessary at any given time. If it is not important, this objection may be disregarded.

There are many factors in favor of sliding doors. As we said, they are easy to make and install. Also, they permit the use of materials too thin to be practical for hinged doors. The making of a sliding door involves no more than cutting a ready-made slab material to length and width. Installation is a question of forming grooves or attaching tracks. Hardware required may be as simple as a set of flush pulls.

Plywood, hardboard, particleboard, laminates—all make good sliding doors, and since these are available in softwoods, hardwoods, and plastics and, in some materials, with a variety of surface textures, you have an easy means of enhancing the appearance of a project. Some materials, such as glass, which would be extremely difficult for the homecraftsman to hang on hinges, become available as door material when you think of them as sliding units.

SLIDING DOORS ARE EASY TO MAKE AND INSTALL

The simplest way to install sliding doors is to cut twin grooves in the top and bottom of the case. The wall that separates the grooves should not be thinner than ⅛", but it should not be so thick that it wastes space.

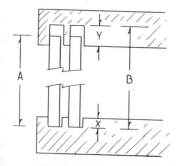

To make sliding doors removable, follow this simple formula: Y equals 2X; A equals B minus X.

Grooves for sliding doors also may be cut in the frontal frame of the case, if one is used. Depth of the grooves should be kept to a minimum so as not to weaken the material.

Glass, for example, especially if the edges are ground, can do quite well in wooden tracks or grooves cut in the case. For more durability, or smoother action if necessary, you can use metal tracks that you can buy. These may be surface-mounted or recessed in grooves so they are less visible.

Sliding doors seldom require lock-or-catch hardware and then it's usually installed for security reasons. And we have already mentioned the fact that, unlike hinged doors, sliding doors do not require "swing" and so cut down on the amount of room needed *around* a project after it's moved from the shop to the house.

Grooves for sliding doors can be formed right in the case members, or in a frontal frame if one is used. The grooves do not have to be deep; often ⅛″ is sufficient. Width of the grooves should be a little more than the thickness of the door stock so the doors will move easily. To make sliding doors removable, the top groove must be deeper than the bottom one. This makes sense for two reasons: it is conceivable that you may wish to remove the doors;

You can form the grooves for sliding doors by attaching cleats, as at left, or with specially made track of wood or metal available at most building-supply stores.

and it will not be necessary to install the doors when you are assembling the case members—you merely add them at the tail-end of the job.

Grooves are needed at the top and the bottom; they are not necessary at the sides and so are often omitted there. But running the grooves completely around will pay off in two ways: all door edges, except the center ones, will be encased in grooves when the doors are closed, creating a dust seal; and the side groove will help conceal any distracting gaps when a door is carelessly closed.

Special sliding-door hardware, consisting of metal tracks and wheels, is available but is necessary mostly on closets and large built-ins. With accessory materials of this type, complete instructions for correct installation are included in the package.

If you want sliding doors to be flush with the edge of the case, form a tongue in the door edge which rides in a matching groove in the case. This necessitates using thicker material for the doors than usual as there must be ample surface to cut the tongue.

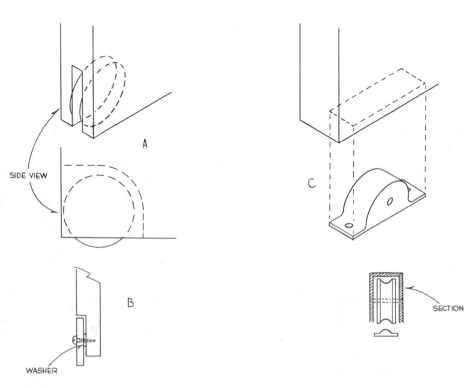

Sliding doors can be equipped with wheels for smoother action. You can make the wheels of plastic or metal and install them in slots cut in each end of the door (A); or you can cut a short rabbet at each end of the door and install the wheel (B). Ready-made tracking systems are available with cased wheels that are inserted in mortises, roll on a special track (C).

Sliding door pulls can be simply finger-tip holes near the edge of each door (left). However, flush pulls, which can be bought, make a neater job (right). These are installed by forcing them into holes cut for the purpose.

CUT DOWN ON SWING SPACE WITH FOLDING DOORS

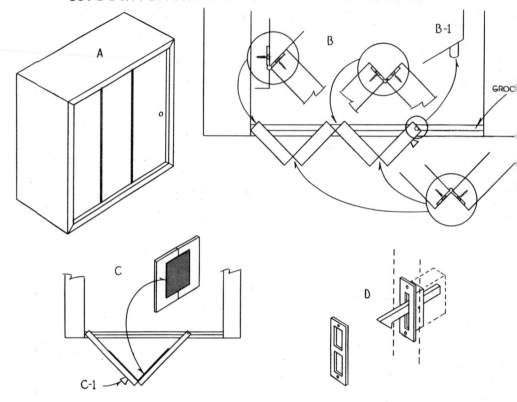

A. Folding doors are vertical panels that move like accordion pleats. **B.** You can make folding doors with any slab material and butt hinges. Note hinge placement and mortising. Guide pin (B-1) rides in a groove at top and bottom of case. **C.** For narrower openings, a two-panel door is sufficient. Here you can use glued-on canvas or self-adhesive felt instead of hinges. **D.** Folding doors can be held closed with this type of catch.

FOLDING DOORS. Folding doors seem more practical for large openings in closets, built-ins, passageways between rooms, and for use as dividers between living areas. When considering such applications it is best to buy the special installation hardware which is available and to follow the instructions supplied with it. You can make your own hollow-core slabs or buy narrow, ready-made doors to hinge for folding. You can even buy a ready-to-install unit, a covered, special mechanism which folds like an accordion so that even a large door occupies very little space when closed. On furniture, the folding door does not require the swing space needed by hinged doors and, when open, will reveal more of the project's contents than possible with sliding doors.

Basically, folding doors are made by hinging vertical pieces so they may fold back on each other. The outside piece is hinged to the case side; the inside piece is pinned to ride a groove cut in the case. On small projects you can get away with a single groove cut in the case bottom; on larger projects it's best to use a groove at the top also. It's also possible to use a track at the top with a T-shaped pin in the door. Thus, the door would actually hang from, and be supported by, the track.

On small projects the pin-and-groove technique works fine and, actually, it is recommended that such designs be confined to small openings so that the hinge on the case will be ample to support the weight of the sections. The pin, then, acts merely as a guide. On long openings it's a good idea to install a pin at the top of every second vertical piece; this will help to insure a folding action.

DROP DOORS. Drop doors can be handy when you don't have swing room for hinged doors and when sliding (or folding doors) won't do, but a more usual application for a drop door is typified by a wall-hung desk where the door drops down to become the writing surface. On other projects a drop door can provide a serving area.

There are three basic methods of installation: hinges, plus hardware to hold the door horizontal; combination hardware which supplies the hinge action and also acts as a stop; and hinges plus a particular case design so the door will stay horizontal without additional hardware.

It is important to judge just how much weight the door must hold. Hardware can be light or heavy, so you can choose it to support just the weight of the door, or the weight of a person who will lean on it while writing.

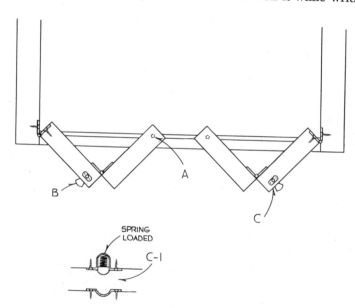

Bi-fold doors open away from each other. Hinges connecting the doors to the case must be mortised, but the panel-joint hinges may be surface-mounted. Guide-pin (A) is also used, but unless doors are very large and heavy only one—at the bottom—is necessary. Pull (B) should be located at this position on each door. Bullet catch (C) is recommended here. C-1 shows catch in cross-section.

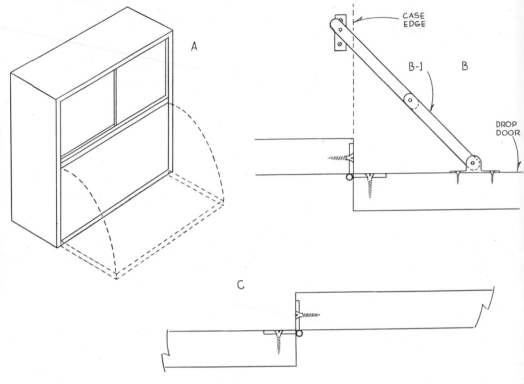

Drop door is most often used on a secretary or small wall-hung desk (A). Door may be on outside edge of case (B), with hinges placed as shown. Folding metal support (B-1) is usually used. When door is flush with or recessed inside frame, hinges must be placed as shown at C.

TAMBOUR DOORS. Tambour doors have a sliding action but are made by assembling vertical slats on a flexible backing so they can actually slide in a curved groove or even in a full circle. They have a clean, uncluttered look and, like other sliding doors, do not require swing space. They require a groove at both the top and the bottom of the opening and, like a conventional sliding door, can be removable if you make the top groove deeper than the bottom one.

Grooves (at top and bottom) must match perfectly if the doors are to work smoothly. The best idea is to form a pattern (actually a guide-template) which may be used with a router on both top and bottom components. If you are not equipped to form the grooves, you can get by with tracks cut on a bandsaw, jigsaw or by hand.

As the door is moved, each slat runs tangential to the curve, so you can see there is a very definite relationship between thickness of the slat, width of the groove, radius of the curve, and width of the slat. The narrower and thinner the slat, the smaller the curve-radius can be. As it is seldom practical to consider a radius of less than 1½", this is a good starting point. To plan for your own needs, make a full-size plan view and plot the curve; then you can easily determine the maximum dimensions of the slats. If you have a particular slat material on hand, then simply reverse the procedure. However, it's best to form slats that will fit a practical curve.

Slats can be as simple as flat pieces of wood which you cut from solid stock, or they can be ready-made mouldings or batten strips. Screen-door mouldings and half-round mouldings are two suggestions worthy of investigating for the purpose.

The conventional method of assembling tambour doors calls for canvas and glue. Best bet is to apply the glue to the canvas, wait for it to become tacky, and then place the slats. Of course, it is important that you avoid getting glue between the slats since they must not be attached to each other except by means of the backing canvas. One method we have used with good success is to substitute a self-adhesive felt for the canvas. This material is available in what used to be five-and-ten-cent stores and in craft-and-hobby shops. Since it is pressure-sensitive it eliminates the gooey glue procedure, and—equally important—the door is ready for installation immediately.

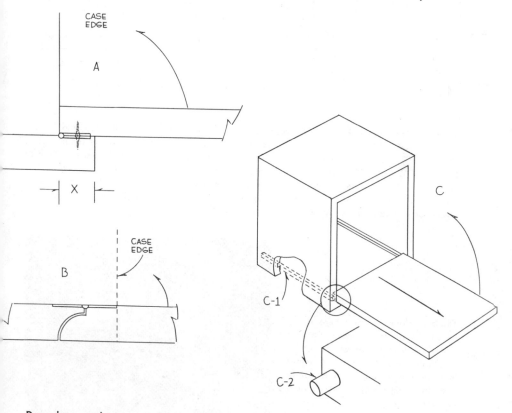

Drop door can be supported without using hardware by (A) providing an overhang (X) on which the door can rest, or (B) shaping the edges in an inverted drop-leaf design. You can also build a combination drop-slide door (C) by cutting a groove (C-1) at the lower sides of the case in which a pivot dowel on the door (C-2) rides. When door is fully extended, it can be tilted into closed position and held by a bullet catch.

TAMBOUR DOORS DISAPPEAR AS THEY ARE OPENED

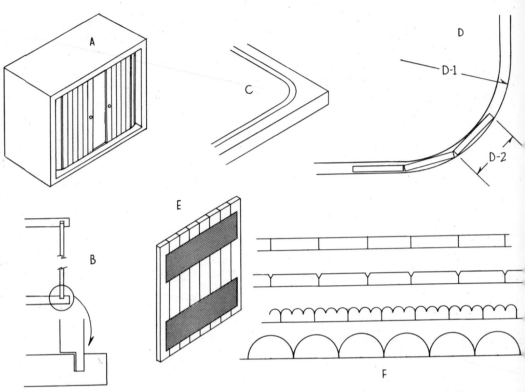

Tambour doors are made of thin slats that slide in curved grooves in the top and bottom of the case (A). Depth of grooves and shape of door edge (B) follow principle of sliding doors. The big difference is the curve in the groove (C). The radius of the turn (D-1) and the width of the slats (D-2), as well as their thickness, must be in proper proportion so that the door has enough freedom to slide smoothly. The slats are assembled with canvas glued across the back (E), or you can use self-adhesive felt. Slats can be square or have chamfered or rounded edges, or you can use ready-made mouldings (F).

Tambour door is shown here riding in bottom groove of case. Backing material is a substitute for a multitude of hinges, keeps slats butted together in a flexible assembly. It is vitally important that top and bottom grooves match.

Be sure to square the slats before you apply the backing. A good way to do this is to place them face-down in the corner formed by the two legs of a carpenter's square. The edge of the first slat rests against one leg of the square, one end of each of the other slats butts against the other leg of the square. If any gaps occur between the slats, you'll know before gluing that the long edges on some of the slats are not parallel. Thus, a correction can be made immediately.

LOUVERED DOORS. Louvered doors may serve merely for appearance or to permit ventilation. In either case, the louvers are placed horizontally in a frame. If the louvers are fixed, they may be set in dadoes cut in the frame pieces. If they are moveable they may be pinned at each end so they can pivot about a central axis. It's not likely that you might ever want to adjust

DRESS UP A CABINET WITH ORIGINAL DOOR STYLES

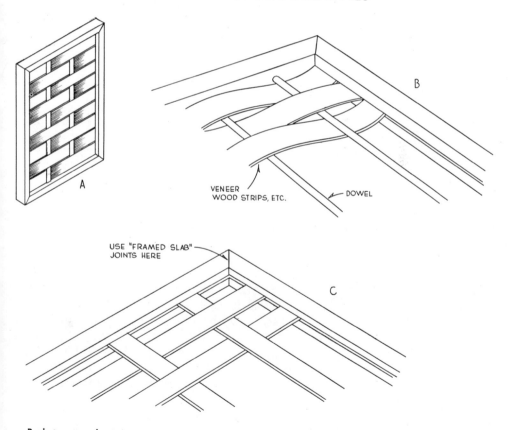

Basket-weave doors are attractive and easy to make. They can be woven of strips of wood, veneer, plastic or cloth set in a grooved frame (A). You can weave the strips through dowels set in the frame (B), or you can make a two-way open weave (C) for a novel effect.

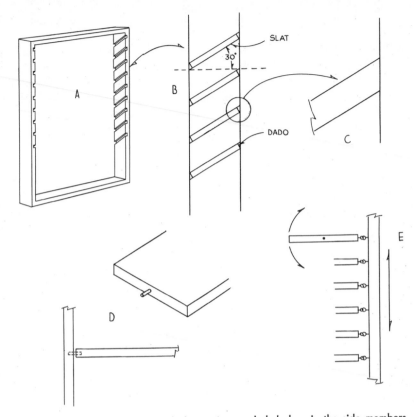

Stationary louver doors are made by cutting angled dadoes in the side members of the door frame (A). Dadoes should be angled at about 30 degrees and the louvers spaced so that the top edge of one louver is on the same line as the bottom edge of the one above (B). Edges of louvers may be beveled so they are flush with the case edge (C) for a neater appearance. Movable louvers (D) are pivoted on a dowel or cut-off nail, opened and closed by a bar tied to the front of each louver with a screw eye (E).

individual louvers; usually, the strips are tied together with a cloth tape or a slim, wooden bar so they may move together. Follow the drawings for essential details.

DOOR HARDWARE. It is quite possible to discover a set of hardware which is so attractive and so intriguing that it inspires you to build a project on which to hang it. Some Oriental styles rely heavily on large, brass fixtures to help create the over-all effect.

Hardware *is* necessary on many projects, so you must choose it for function. It can perform unobtrusively or it can supply decorative details. Many times shaping a particular area of a component substitutes for hardware. This is especially true on drawer and door pulls.

Aside from the guidance provided by the laws of harmony and good taste, it it difficult to set down hard and fast rules concerning the choice and the use of hardware. When making a reproduction or working along the lines dictated by a particular furniture style, the choice is made for you. You simply use the hardware called for. For example, you can buy pulls and knobs that are exactly right for Chippendale, French styles, English Regency, Provincial and Contemporary. Many of these may be adapted to styling which is not truely authentic.

You can be more flexible when choosing fixtures for original designs; often the choice is one of personal preference and taste and of the project-image which you see in your own mind. Cleated board doors with a cabinet-door lip can be mounted with semiconcealed, offset hinges, but since such an assembly is easily associated with rough-hewn and rustic styling, wrought-iron strap hinges would also be compatible.

The project material, to a considerable degree, will automatically influence your choice. Of course this is perfectly logical since you already knew the styling you had in mind or the effect you wished to create before you decided on what material to use. If you were making a dining-room set along provincial lines and decided on knotty pine, you would end up choosing provincial hardware. Sleek, hardwood plywood automatically affects styling and thus influences hardware selection.

Probably the one rule you can apply generally is to decide whether the hardware is going to be prominent or subdued. You can use a pull on a drawer or a door and it will not attract too much attention, but you can also back up that pull with a fancy escutcheon plate and thus call more attention to it. A cabinet-door lock can function with just a simple hole for the key to enter, or you can use a keyhole escutcheon. Of course, what may appear to be a purely decorative addition may actually serve a very practical function. Escutcheon plates are good examples of this—on a pull or knob they protect the surrounding area and keep it clean; on a keyhole they do the same job.

CHAPTER SIXTEEN

CABINET BACKS AND DIVIDERS

A BACK on a cabinet or a chest will dust-proof it and will add strength. On some projects, such as a chest of drawers, you never see the back. On others the back is revealed each time you open a door.

The attachment of the back is not critical so far as strength is concerned unless you have a large case without shelves, frames, or dividers. In this case the back *can* supply rigidity.

Two simple methods of attaching cabinet backs are shown here. At left, the back is attached to cleats which are glued and nailed to the inside surfaces of the case members. At right, the back is butted against the back edges of the case. Note that the back is cut slightly smaller than the outside dimensions of the case so it will not be visible from the front.

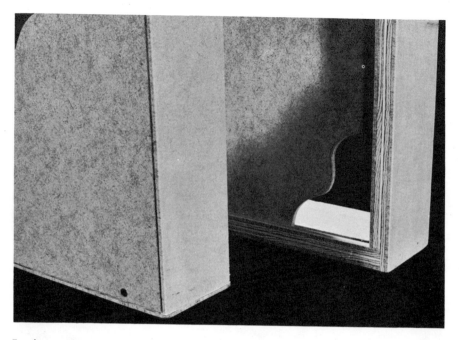

For those wishing to take the trouble, here are two advanced methods of adding a back. At left, the back is let into rabbets cut in the case members, while at right the back is let into grooves. The latter method requires that the back is assembled with the sides.

Generally, the material does not have to be as pretty to look at as that used in more prominent pieces. An exception might be a project which will also serve as a divider of some sort. An example could be a bookcase, placed to direct traffic through a room. In such cases, the back should be "pretty" since it will be seen as often as the front.

Materials used can be thin slabs of plywood, hardboard or particleboard. Thickness rarely runs over ¼″, while ⅛″, especially in a stiff hardboard, is used quite frequently.

Don't overlook the use of materials like perforated hardboards. These are quite practical on projects that house units that give off heat—radios and hi-fi components. Also, a tall divider-project with such a back provides a ready means of hanging decorative accessories.

Dividers in a case, either vertical or horizontal, are usually set in dadoes cut in opposite case members. It is important to locate these cuts correctly before assembly begins. If you do not have the tools for cutting dadoes, you can buy small metal channels that are hammered into the sides of the case and hold ¼″ dividers of hardboard or plywood.

When dividers are visible from the front of the case, it is a good idea to conceal the dado cuts or the metal channels with a front frame. This, as has been seen, not only hides the dadoes for the dividers but also the joints used at the corners of the case.

Vertical dividers in this hi-fi cabinet, seen here with sliding doors removed, are made of hardboard and fit in dadoes cut in the top and bottom case members. Dado cuts must match accurately if dividers are to be straight.

CHAPTER SEVENTEEN

SHELVES

THE THINGS you plan to store or display are important factors affecting shelf design. It doesn't much matter whether you are hanging the shelves on a wall, putting them in a free-standing bookcase, or installing them in a cabinet or chest; you must consider the items they will hold in order to use the shelves conveniently and to get maximum space utilization. A series of equally spaced, horizontal slabs is seldom the most efficient answer. Consider books. Eight inches is a good shelf depth (width of slab used) for the average novel but for some books, 12″ is better. Book height is not the only factor to consider when establishing space between shelves; you must also allow for finger room so it's easy to get books out. Spacing of 12″ seems adequate for general use but some books will require more and many will require less. So book shelves should either be adjustable or designed to provide for the variations you will

"Floating" shelves are supported by iron rods which are inserted through the wall covering and into the wall studs. Back edge of shelf is drilled to fit over rods. Accurate drilling and good, flat stock are critical factors in getting neat results.

You can make your own shelf supports of wood . . .

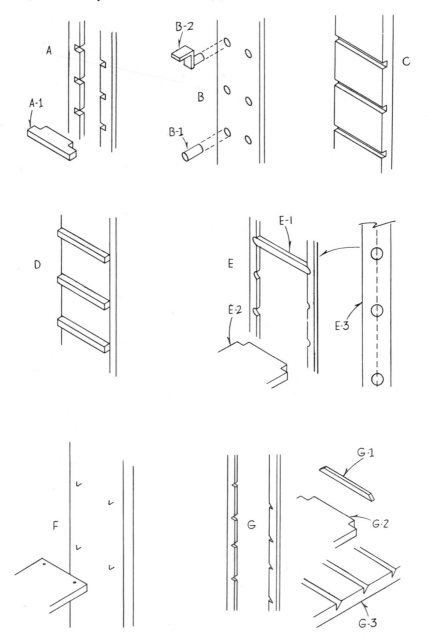

A. Notched strips receive shaped shelf brackets (A-1), or ends of shelves may be so cut and fit into the notches. B. Short dowels (B-1) or ready-made clips (B-2) fit in blind holes and support shelves. C. Shelves fit in dadoes cut in side supports. D. Shelves rest on cleats attached to sides. E. Instead of notches, half-round cuts are fitted with shaped brackets (E-1) on which shelves (E-2) rest. Easy way to make strips is to drill a series of holes, then cut on center line (E-3). F. Shelves are drilled to fit on L-shaped hooks. G. Similar to A and E except cuts are triangular. Brackets (G-1) fit into cuts, and shelves (G-2) rest on brackets. For production runs, make V cuts across board (G-3), then cut into individual strips.

Or use ready-made hardware . . .

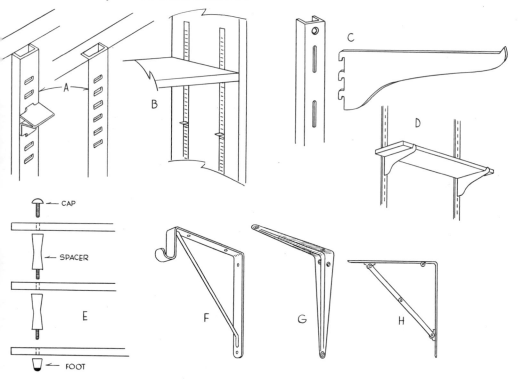

A. Metal wall strip with adjustable clips—can be attached on surface or let into vertical grooves so shelf is flush with sides (B). C. Another type of metal strip, takes shelf brackets— usually used on walls (D). E. Spacers with threaded dowels that fit through holes in shelves allow you to add as many shelves as you have spacers. F. Shelf bracket for closets also holds clothes pole. G. Simple iron shelf bracket for use where appearance is not important. H. Hinged bracket allows shelf, or table, to be folded out of the way.

encounter. These considerations point up the value of designing for what you are going to store or display before you start building.

Another bad design feature of fixed and equally spaced shelves is that you limit storage height to that one distance between shelves. By thinking about step shelves, balcony shelves, and triangular shelves (as the drawings show) you provide for storage of items at various heights and the items will be more convenient to get to.

Don't guess at spacing and shelf-depths. When you make a storage project, you know pretty well what you will be using it for. Then you can design by actually measuring the items and by pre-arranging them for space utilization and convenience.

The following section is devoted to a discussion of the various types of furniture you may want to build—tables, desks, cabinets, chests, chairs and bed frames. Most of the relevant construction techniques have already been covered in previous chapters; now we shall be concerned with dimensions, styles and special problems. Included in this section are photographs of many commercial pieces on the market today, in Early American, Contemporary and Traditional styles. They are not intended to serve as models for you to copy exactly, but to suggest ideas, both in design and construction, which you might apply to your own projects.

Part Four—THE FURNITURE

CHAPTER EIGHTEEN

TABLES

MAKE ONE table and you've made them all. This is a fairly realistic general comment when you stop to consider that every table is basically a slab plus four legs, with the possible addition of rails and stretchers. Usually it is only size and decorative details that distinguish one from another, if we assume a uniform degree of craftsmanship. Play tables, dining tables, coffee tables, step tables, end tables, occasional tables—all are pretty simple unless you choose to make them tough. Granted, of course, that styling can affect time and effort required in construction—a French Provincial table will require more shop time than a flush door mounted on ready-made wrought-iron legs— but nevertheless the concept is still the same. All of the practical considerations apply no matter what kind of table you are building.

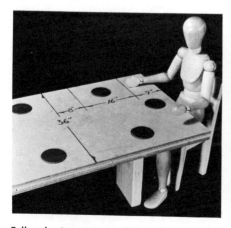 

Follow basic spacing at left in designing any table. Allowing 16″ per place with 8″ in between, a table for eight should be 36″ by 82″. For round tables, 36″ is the minimum top diameter for four people, 48″ for six. Space per person is same as for rectangular tables.

These factory-made contemporary tables, inspired by Danish design, combine simplicity of construction with graceful styling. They are perfect examples of slab-leg-rail construction. You can improvise on these basic designs to suit your own taste by applying the construction techniques already covered in previous chapters.

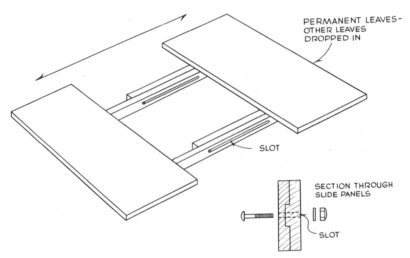

A simple method of making an extension table for insert leaves. The rails are slotted and held with a bolt, washer and nut. A tongue cut the length of one rail slides in a groove cut in the other. Legs may be attached to the rails in any of the prescribed ways.

Table size is not arbitrary. This is one design job where function almost dictates proportions, So that a person can sit and eat comfortably, dining-table height must be such that he can be well above the surface yet have adequate knee room. The top must be sized to give elbow room for each person the table is to accommodate, plus space for dishes and silver.

The sturdiness of a table and its life span depend on the way the legs are attached. Structurally, it's here that the table is constantly tested. Every time you move or use a table (or somebody sits on it) the leg-to-top joint gets the strain. But, of course, this is not an insurmountable problem. Just picture the top as a span that must support weight. The biggest safety factor is in minimum slant on the legs. The closer to zero the slant, the stronger the assembly.

The strongest method of assembling a table is the common leg-and-rail design. What this does is establish a strong, open frame (composed of legs and rails) to which the top slab is attached. The frame joint can be reinforced by using corner blocks, but these are most likely to be needed in higher tables (dining tables as opposed to coffee tables) and in designs where the legs slant in two directions. One trick is to cut the corner block so it fits snugly against the leg but not against the rails. If you screw to the leg first and then the rails, you'll be pulling everything in nice and tight.

The mortise-tenon joint and the dowel joint are most often used. Whichever you choose don't forget to set the rail back from the edge of the leg. A hairline joint crack, which will often develop at this point, won't be noticeable then.

Attaching legs directly to the top slab is not as good, as far as strength is

Hale Co., Inc.

This is a typical drop-leaf table which also has an extension top. Built of maple, it measures 42″ by 24″ closed, but with drop leaves raised and insert leaves in place lengthens to 82″. Courtesy *Furniture World*.

Leister's of Hanover, Pa.

Trestle drop-leaf end table in white pine has a single husky stretcher attached to the legs with through tenons held with small blocks. Legs and feet, cut separately from heavy stock, could be attached with dowel joints.

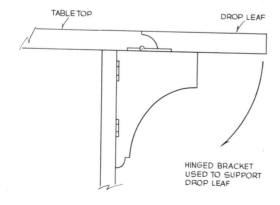

Hinged wooden brackets are one method of supporting the leaves of a drop-leaf table. Brackets may be hinged to the rails, which would have to be somewhat wider than usual. When the leaves are down, the brackets fold against the rails.

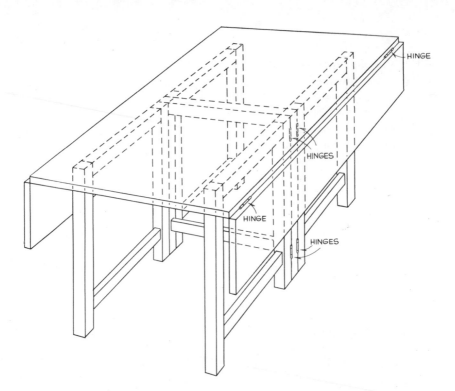

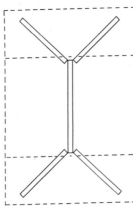

Here is an idea for a drop-leaf table with gate legs to support the leaves. The legs are frame assemblies hinged to a center frame which swing out and under the leaves when the table is opened, as shown in the top-view diagram at left.

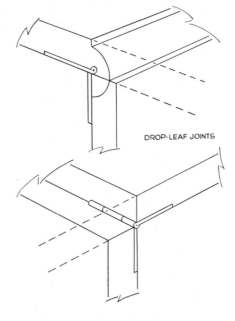

DROP-LEAF JOINTS

Two kinds of drop-leaf joints are shown here. The top one requires routing the edges of both pieces so the leaf edge fits neatly over the table edge when the leaf is raised. The bottom joint is simpler—table and leaf edges are left square and the two pieces hinged as shown.

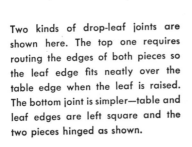

This contemporary cocktail table, 34" in diameter and 15" high, is covered with plastic laminate in a wood-grain pattern. Any of the slab-to-leg techniques are applicable here, with dowel stretchers used to brace the legs.

Baumritter Corp.

Baumritter Corp.

Baumritter Corp.

Simple to build yet appropriate in any room of modern furniture, this lamp table is a slab-to-leg construction, with dowels between the stretchers creating a novel magazine rack. The top, covered in walnut plastic laminate, is 17" by 25"; the table stands 22" high.

Adding a smaller slab to the preceding table, and eliminating the magazine rack, creates a new piece. Shaped dowels glued in blind holes support the step, and smaller dowels form the stretchers. The surface is covered with white plastic laminate.

Haywood-Wakefield Co.

A fresh treatment of the leg-and-rail assembly is seen in this contemporary end table. The square legs and side bandings are of rock maple, the top and sides of solid cherry. Miter joints were used to join the top and sides, creating a continuous flow of grain and a neat edge. Courtesy *Furniture World*.

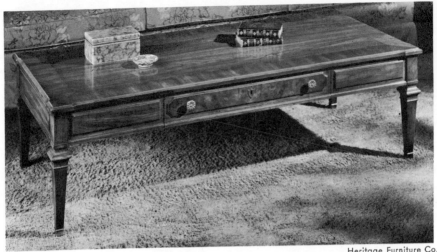

Traditional style calls for more intricate work and fine materials. This rectangular cocktail table is made of cherry, but despite the seemingly complex design is basically a slab-rail-legs assembly. Construction details for installing a drawer through a rail are shown in the accompanying drawing. The table is 56″ long, 25″ wide and 16″ high.

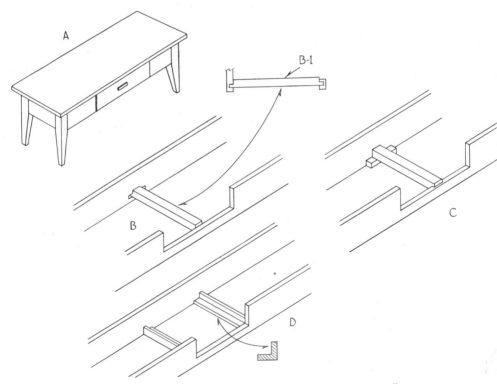

To provide for a drawer through the front rail of a table (A), you can install a center runner (B), which is rabbeted at the ends and fits in slots in the front and rear rails (B-1). Or you can eliminate the slots and rabbet only one end of the runner, which is glued to the edge of the front rail, supported at the rear by a small block glued and screwed to the back rail (C). A simpler method, but providing a less efficient guide for the drawer, is to use L-shaped pieces on either side of the drawer opening (D).

concerned, as using the leg-rail design, but for smaller and lower tables it is quite satisfactory. Ready-made legs are often equipped with hardware that gives maximum attachment strength.

When you make legs, you can often increase strength by assembling the legs first to cross-cleats and then attaching the cleats to the underside of the slab. Straight legs can be made to slant out by shaping the cleat like a wedge. And there is another way, if you wish to do without the cleat: you can make individual wedge-shaped mounting blocks for the legs. The wedge provides the leg slant, and by positioning the mounting block accordingly you can determine whether the leg will slant in one direction or two.

Stretchers are often used to reinforce table legs, but you must be careful on dining tables since they can interfere with sitting up close. Most often, cross-stretchers are used since they do the job without interfering with the sitters.

A table slab can shrink ¼″ or more. If you attach it so the natural shrinkage will be resisted by the rails or the leg-rail assembly, the slab may crack or even distort the entire assembly. Ever discover after a table has been in use a few months that the legs suddenly seem uneven? That's why most solid-top tables are attached with little angle clips that hold the top in place but do not restrict its natural tendency to contract and expand with atmospheric changes. This holds particularly true for solid-lumber tops. It will be apparent to a lesser extent in plywood slabs and in slabs made from flush doors or

Nest of tables in traditional style is basically a slab-leg-rail construction, the two largest tables having only three rails. You could modify the decorative details according to your own taste, skill and equipment.

Heritage Furniture Co.

Shrinkage is a critical factor in slab-to-rail assembly. Do not glue the slab to the rails; if the slab shrinks it will crack, or distort the table. Two basic methods of attaching a top slab to rails are shown here. At left, metal clips set in grooves in the rail and screwed to the slab give it plenty of leeway. At right, screws are driven through the rails into the slab and counterbored.

If you want a glass top, have the glass cut and polished by a professional. This is not a job for the average home shop. The table can be designed so the glass is framed by the rails (left). Make the rabbet cuts just a fraction deeper than the thickness of the glass. Legs can be screwed to a glass top by using rubber grommets in the holes (right). Cement small wooden buttons on top to hide the grommets and screws.

hollow-core slabs that you make yourself. When legs are individually attached, the slab can move at will but even here, should the slab distort slightly, it can cause unevenness in the legs.

Good finishing does much to minimize this condition; filling and sealing especially. But if this is to be of maximum help, it should be done on the underside of the slab as well as the top.

Most of the considerations discussed in previous sections concerning slab construction, leg shapes, and methods of leg attachment apply to table projects. (See Chapter 11, BROAD SURFACES—SLABS; Chapter 12, LEGS.) Other, more specific ideas and considerations are shown in the sketches and photos in this section.

CHAPTER NINETEEN

DESKS

PROBABLY THE first "desk" was a table, and it came to be known as a "writing table" because that's what it was used for. Even now, the real difference between a "desk" and a "table" lies in the components on which the slab rests; the design of these is determined by the function of the unit.

A desk that will be used in a bedroom and mostly for answering social letters doesn't have to be more than a small slab on legs with a few shallow drawers. This is adequate since all you'll need to store is some writing paper and envelopes, stamps and writing implements. Such a unit is more a writing table than a desk.

But change the location of the desk and its function and see what happens. Say it's a desk for the den where the man of the house may occasionally have to do some business homework and where household records will be stored. Now the slab must be larger and its storage capacity must be increased. Instead of legs, the slab will have to rest on drawer units which are actually small chests. This so you will have more compartments to provide storage for additional materials and, possibly, to include one or two file draw-

A desk is basically a slab on legs—with or without drawers . . .

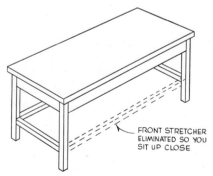

FRONT STRETCHER
ELIMINATED SO YOU
SIT UP CLOSE

Put a slab on two chests and a desk becomes more functional . . .

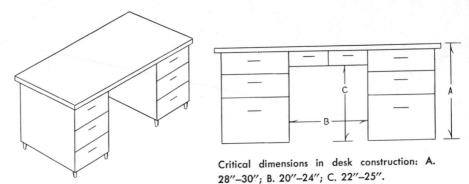

Critical dimensions in desk construction: A. 28"–30"; B. 20"–24"; C. 22"–25".

Use one back to connect twin chests . . . or put individual backs on the chests and connect them with the slab . . .

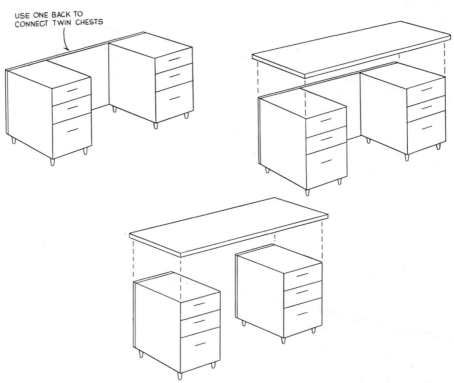

USE ONE BACK TO CONNECT TWIN CHESTS

ers. Design the desk for a student and, again, the needs of the user will make it necessary to go beyond the scope of the basic writing table.

Regardless of the detailing there are certain basic dimensions which are generally applicable. Whether it's a desk or a table, it must be comfortable for writing. Thus the total height falls between 28" and 30". To write comfortably you must be able to sit close. Thus you leave the "kneehole." There is

Chests may be built of solid or post-and-panel slabs—but eliminate the top . . .

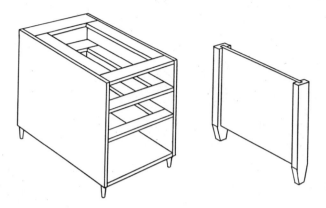

Chest may rest on bottom, on round or shaped legs, on a frame . . .

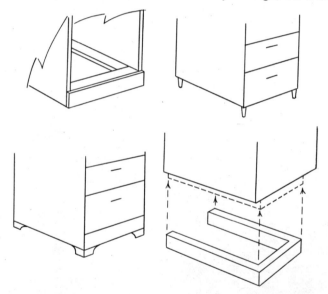

You can use smaller chests and longer legs . . . or you can use only one chest, one pair of legs . . .

The pencil drawer can hang from the slab . . .

Or you can use an open frame and guide-runner system for the drawer . . .

The component system of furniture building is perfectly exemplified by this modern factory-made desk. Composed of a slab, a pedestal and four legs, it is an ideal design for the home-craftsman's consideration. The top measures 24″ by 54″.

These Early American style pedestal desks suggest several design ideas. The desk at right is two-faced, one side of the pedestals containing drawers, the other side bookshelves. It measures 56″ by 26″ by 30½″ high. Desk at left is 50″ by 24″ by 30″ high.

Another two-faced desk, this one of modern Danish design, in rosewood, has drawers on one side of the cases, drop doors and shelves on the other. It is essentially a slab-rail-leg construction with the cases hung from the rails. Courtesy *Furniture World*.

some freedom here but the space you provide shouldn't be less than 22″ high or less than 20″ wide. This is for average use. If you are making the desk for a child, then the minimum specifications can be less.

The length and width of the slab also deserve some practical consideration. You should be able to reach all areas of the surface without having to leave the chair and without having to stretch. These considerations actually enable you to establish a slab dimension which will be just right for you.

Sit in a chair as if you were sitting at a desk. Stretch your right arm forward and measure from your chest to the tips of your fingers. This can be the width of the slab. In the same position, stretch both arms out in line with your shoulders and measure the span. This will give you the maximum length of the

This reproduction of an old Master's desk would make an interesting homeshop project. It features a lift-top storage compartment, slide-out board and a bookcase on the reverse side of the pedestal. Note the use of contrasting dowels on the drawer fronts, legs and storage bin. Dimensions are 58" by 26¼" by 37¼" high. Courtesy *Furniture World*.

Drop-lid desk in maple is really a modified chest of drawers, the case sides being cut on an angle above the third drawer and a drop door installed. The sides of the case are slabs of glued-up lumber. Dimensions are 32" by 17" by 40" high. Courtesy *Furniture World*.

slab. Even this practical approach to suitable dimensions isn't foolproof since, from the sitting position, you won't be able to reach the left and right outboard corners of the slab. To accomplish this the slab would have to be shorter than your span or the design would have to be semicircular or kidney-shaped.

The best way to "see" the construction of a desk, is to picture the components as separate units. Thus you have a slab which sits on legs (writing table) or small drawer units (desk).

Drawer units should be closed at the back but are left open at the top since the slab itself is adequate cover. It's much more convenient to build the components as separate assemblies. Afterwards the slab can be attached by means of dowels, or screws or even small metal angles. All of the details for the construction of desk components—slabs, drawers, chests, etc.—are shown elsewhere in this book. (See Chapter 11, BROAD SURFACES—SLABS; Chapter 12, LEGS; Chapter 13, RAILS AND FRAMES; Chapter 14, DRAWERS.)

CHAPTER TWENTY

CABINETS AND CHESTS

WHEN IS a chest a chest and when should you call it a cabinet or a case? Some furniture catalogs identify products with drawers as chests and say cabinet when doors are involved. Often an almost identical piece, previously called a chest, becomes a dresser, a bureau, even a "server." A hope chest is a box with a hinged lid, but these days some items made to serve the same purpose are made like a chest-of-drawers. No doubt, the primary use of the item (and the talents of the sales force) have much to do with the listings,

A chest is basically an open box. It may be . . .

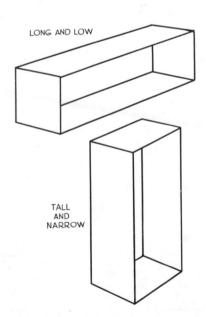

LONG AND LOW

TALL
AND
NARROW

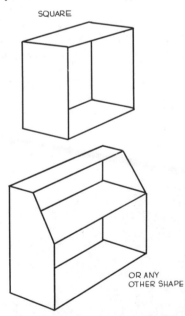

SQUARE

OR ANY
OTHER SHAPE

It may stand on its own bottom . . . or on legs . . .

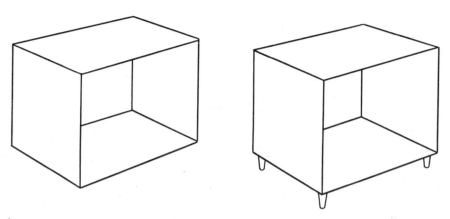

It may rest on a frame with legs . . . or the legs may be an extension of the sides . . .

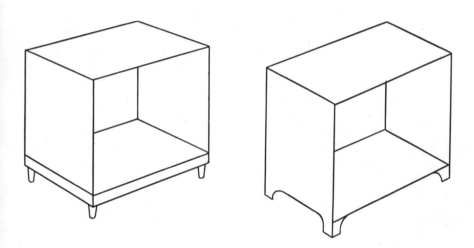

Add shelves for a bookcase . . . drawers for a chest . . . or doors for a cabinet . . .

Add a top unit and a case becomes a hutch, or a china closet . . .

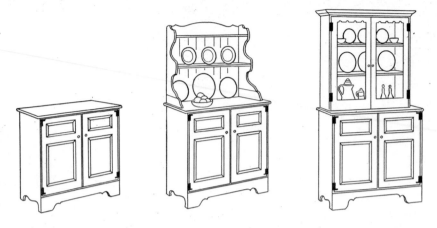

Enlarge the size of the case to make a buffet . . . which also can become a hutch . . .

but for our purposes let's accept the fact that all these various products do have one thing in common—the basic form is a "case." Which is one reason why, logically enough, they are all grouped under the heading of "case-goods."

Simply, a case is a box stood on one of its sides or an end. If you place a well-made drawer so its bottom becomes a back and its face becomes a top-slab, you have a pretty good picture of a basic case form which serves as a model for a good percentage of storage furniture.

Hang it on a wall after installing shelves and hanging doors and you have a kitchen cabinet. Fit it with horizontal frames and install drawers and you have a chest-of-drawers. Use shelves and set it on the floor and you have a bookcase. Design shelves for hi-fi components and some vertical racks for record storage, maybe introduce a low table or bench for it to sit on, and you have a hi-fi cabinet. Of course, it becomes a stereo cabinet if you have stereo instead of mono equipment.

146

About 55″ is considered maximum height for a chest. This allows the contents of the top drawers to be easily visible and accessible. Low chests (or cabinets) run from 25″ to 36″ high. Chest depth can be anywhere from 15″ to 21″. Sample dimensions for a modern chest would be 54″ high, 36″ wide, 20″ deep.

Leo H. Spivack, Inc.

This handsome rosewood dresser is composed of two chests. The top one contains shirt drawers masked by a tambour door with vertical grain which contrasts with the horizontal grain in the drawer fronts of the bottom chest. Courtesy *Furniture World*.

By simplifying construction of the doors and the feet, the homecraftsman could build a similar Colonial dry sink. The planting area is copper lined, the decks on either side covered with plastic laminate. Dimensions are 45½″ by 16″ by 35½″ high. Courtesy *Furniture World*.

Built of northern hardwoods and finished in a warm antique tone, this accessory chest measures 23″ by 15½″ by 51″ high. Note how the simple case construction is given a decorative touch at the bottom by a single shaped piece. Courtesy *Furniture World*.

Handsome china-buffet cabinet of northeastern white pine shows how a case combines with a top unit framed to provide for drawers and doors. The piece measures 60″ by 19″ by 84″ high. Courtesy *Furniture World*.

Even the detailing of a quality drawer could be used to represent good case construction: strong, tight joints where the top slab meets the side slabs; an inset back for dust-proofing and for additional rigidity; the bottom (drawer back) let in to the sides to complete what will be a lasting assembly.

The dimensions must be changed to suit it for its purpose; its design must be particular relative to placement. Since we are considering items intended for people to use, they must, like all furniture, be scaled to the size of the human body. Height is more critical than length, width, or depth. Length and width are often influenced by where a piece will be placed. A chest-of-drawers could run the full length of a wall and, if the height is okay, you can still reach the contents of each drawer. But if you made the chest 7′ high, then the top drawers would be difficult to use. What you will store in the project must be considered and will (or should) influence size and thus design.

Make a case for books and the top shelf should not be higher than the

Crawford Mfg. Co.

This maple chest features a drop-lid desk in addition to its ample drawer space. The drop-lid is held closed by magnetic catches. Dimensions are 42″ by 18″ by 46″ high. Courtesy *Furniture World*.

average person, without stepladder, can reach. Ideal height for a chest-of-drawers should permit the contents of the top drawer or drawers to be easily accessible, and visible. A wall-hung case (or cabinet) is like a bookcase; you should be able to reach all the contents without toe-dancing.

Occasionally, you throw the rules away. In a library you install floor-to-ceiling shelves because you want maximum storage even if it means climbing a chair occasionally. Sometimes you go along with less than ideal accessibility simply because the items to be stored won't be needed too often.

In addition to size, which relates to function, placement, human proportions, and the height-length-width of things we use, good design follows the few basic rules we have already discussed, and they apply regardless of whether the style of the project will be Early American or ultra-modern.

One good rule when doing the initial planning is to keep style considerations out of the picture for a while. Visualize the project in its most basic form as slabs and frames. Decisions on legs, types of slabs, etc., can follow. All of the construction details needed to make case-goods projects will be found in those sections dealing with furniture components.

Danish breakfront or hi-fi cabinet has many provocative design ideas. This one is made in rosewood and teak, but the design suggests using plywood for economy and workability in the home shop. Courtesy *Furniture World.*

Leo H. Spivack, Inc.

Stack units solve storage problems and decorate an entire wall. You can build a number of cases and equip them with either open shelves, drawers or doors, then arrange them according to your own taste and needs. Courtesy *Furniture World*.

CHAPTER TWENTY-ONE

CHAIRS

You CAN make a good dining chair with raw materials that consist of nothing more than a length of 2-by-4 and about 1½ square feet of plywood. The material may not sound impressive, but if you consider that a chair is really not much more than a skeleton frame, and if you are inclined to go along with clean and simple styling plus good engineering, there is an important chairmaking lesson in this. Typically, this kind of project brings up visions of an endless and dreary routine of duplication. Well, if you are making a set of

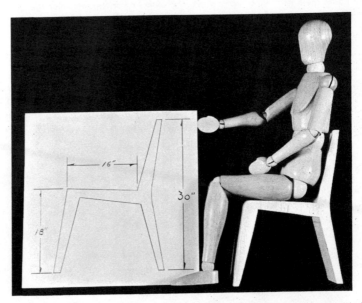

Chairs for tables and desks have the most rigid dimensional standards. Give or take an inch or two, dimensions shown here are fairly typical. The seat width, which should be 17″ or 18″, is important not only for the person using the chdir but determines the number of chairs that will fit at the table.

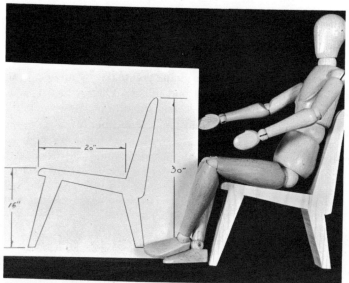

Chairs for relaxation, whether or not they are equipped with arms, can have lower, deeper seats and a sharper-slanting back than desk or table chairs. And they are wider, too, from 20″ to 24″.

six or eight chairs there must be duplication of parts since the chairs themselves will be duplicates, but there is considerable difference between twenty-four cabriole legs and twenty-four straight tapers. And look at the difference between twenty-four legs that you make and six sets of legs that you buy.

The point is that chair-making, like any homeshop woodworking job, need not be discouraging. There is an efficient method for you regardless of whether you own all the tools in the world or just a few of them; regardless of whether you love to live with sawdust or prefer to break up the workshop routine with an occasional game of golf.

Choose a system which is compatible with your equipment and with your incentives. If you own a lathe and love using it, you won't mind turning out twenty-four similar pieces. If you don't own a lathe, or have one but don't enjoy the prospect of so much duplication, and love turned pieces—you can buy them. This is part of the process of planning the project: what you want or need—the extent of your equipment—the extent of your interest—the time available.

DESIGNING A CHAIR. Chairs are for sitting, whether to work, to rest, or to eat. Commercial chairs are designed for the average person and, if you wish to suit persons other than yourself, you too must stick fairly close to standard dimensions. This is especially true of utility chairs used primarily for dining. The taller the sitter the more he will appreciate a seat which is several inches higher (and deeper) than normal since it would suit his leg length. But, when using the chair at a table, he might scrape his knees on the table rail or apron.

Standard dimensions, however, do not limit style or design—a quick look around any furniture store will prove that. The height of the back, the shape of the leg, the size of the seat, the slope of the seat and/or the arms, the basic style—all can be used effectively even though you are working within the limits imposed by necessary standardization.

Remember we are talking of the chairs you make for *anyone* to use. If you are going to give yourself a break and make a chair which is exactly right for you, then use the standard specs as a starting point and modify them to suit your own particular angles, and lengths and bends.

Side chairs (like those you use at a table) are more severe because, as I keep telling my sons, you are not supposed to slump or droop at the table. A secretary needs such a chair if she is to work efficiently at a typewriter.

All the parts for this side chair, except for the back and seat, were cut from a single length of 2-by-4. Shape a 34″-long 2-by-4, then slice it apart to form the two back legs. Split 2-by-4s, too, for the front legs and seat rails. The curve in the back slat can be cut with a bandsaw.

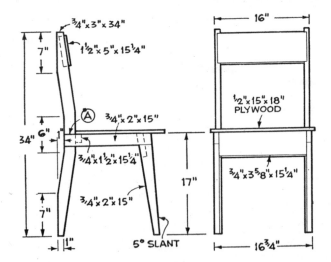

Deeper, wider and lower than the chair on opposite page, this armchair could be used at a desk or dining table. Note that the slant of the legs is visually increased by the taper of the leg from top to bottom.

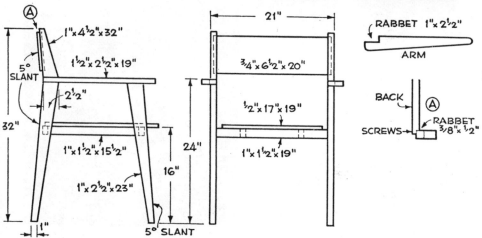

Such a chair is designed so the body assumes two vertical planes and one horizontal one: vertical from foot to knee; horizontal from knee to base of spine; vertical from base of spine to neck.

Armchairs permit a more relaxed attitude. Here, the seats can be lower and deeper. Back and seat slope can be more pronounced. This is a psychological aspect of chair making that can be tested by examining your own reaction to chair types. In a dining chair you sit up straight and proper; in an armchair, even one without upholstery, you are more inclined to relax.

Chair designing seems to bother people and it shouldn't. Remember that a chair is basically a leg-and-rail assembly. The two back legs can extend to become posts which form the chair back. If you remember these two basic points and draw within a form which represents the over-all dimensions of the project your efforts will be successful.

BUILDING A CHAIR. Chair construction is tested most where the legs join the rails and where the back joins the seat. Stress at these points is not great when the legs are straight but does increase considerably when you slant the legs. Another consideration is that most of the sitter's weight is at the back of the chair. On slanted legs, the weight tends to spread the legs even more; hence, greater strain where the leg attaches to the rail or, when rails are not used, where the leg attaches to the seat frame or to the seat itself. Stretchers are often used since they add considerably to the durability of the project. Stretchers can run from back leg to front leg, or between legs, or they can do both. Another system often used is to run stretchers from back leg to front leg and then connect the stretchers in the middle with a single cross-stretcher. In this case the stretchers would form an H shape.

Kingsize chair, designed for a big man, is intended for use in a den or study. It would look out of place in a room with conventionally sized pieces.

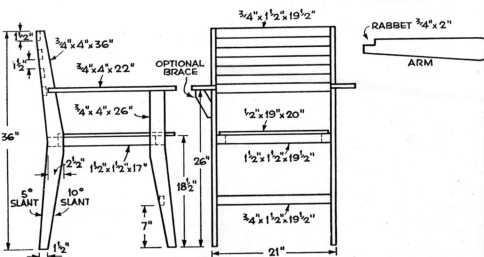

Framework for a semi-upholstered chair. As arms and legs will be left uncovered, the basic chair design doesn't change much. The seat and back will be webbed or fitted with No-Sag springs, padded and covered, before the arm-and-leg assemblies are permanently attached. See next photo for how to shape the heavy curve on the front of the seat.

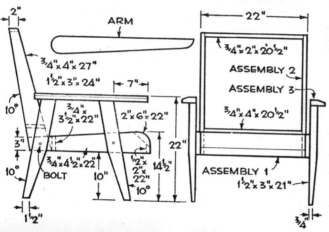

To cut the piece for the front of the chair on a table saw, mark the arc on the end of the stock and make a series of bevel cuts to remove the bulk of the waste material. Very little sanding will be required to form a true arc if you make enough bevel cuts and reset the saw blade after each cut so all cuts will be tangent to the edge of the circle.

Round legs can be used in chair construction for a seat frame rather than a leg-rail assembly. The top of the leg can end in a tenon which fits the hole bored in the corner block. Note the dowel—while it is not spiraled or grooved it is chamfered at each end and indented to provide room for glue and air.

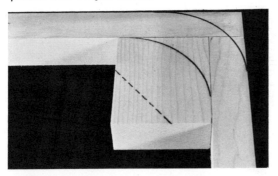

This technique will let you turn a corner while also providing for a seat-attachment block. Parts here are glued together and then shaped after the glue is dry. Solid lines indicate cut for turning corner; dotted line is for the block.

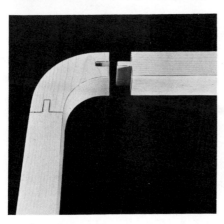

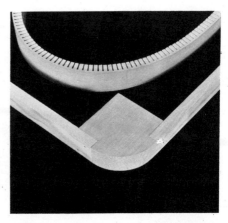

Tongue-and-groove with shaped corner block is a neat way to turn a corner. Best bet is to form the grooves in the corner piece before you shape it. This is a good technique to use for a smooth joint when the seat frame is exposed.

Two other ways to turn a corner: Top is the kerfing technique which can provide for an unbroken line, but it should be reinforced with glue blocks. Bottom shows a block which is shaped to provide for both a round corner and a leg-attachment block.

Joints for Chairs. In the final analysis, the chair, regardless of type, size, or style will be only as strong as the joints used to assemble the parts. In addition to the strength of the joint, consider the appearance. For example, on outdoor furniture the appearance of the joint is not so important. Here, we accept a visible means of joining parts, so screws, lag screws, nuts, and bolts are adequate. On indoor pieces we demand a more exacting craftsmanship and so require hidden joints that still supply the strength. A joint is seldom completely hidden; there is always the line where one part joins another. But the means of keeping the parts together is invisible.

If you wish, you seldom need think beyond a mortise-tenon (or variations of it) or the dowel joint. The mortise-tenon is used widely on commercial pieces since it is strong, but also because manufacturers have the proper equipment. In the home shop, the dowel joint is easier to do, and it will match the mortise-tenon in both strength and appearance.

The critical factor in the dowel joint is the precise location of holes on mating parts. The secret here lies in allotting the necessary time to do an accurate job, and in setting up simple jigs that mechanically locate the hole on multiple pieces. If you have twenty-four legs and each needs two holes on two adjacent surfaces, you would have a difficult time plotting the hole locations on each piece and doing it accurately. It's best to locate the holes on one piece and then to use that sample as a means of clamping blocks of wood to the drill-press table to create a locating-jig so all the other parts will be correctly placed under the spindle. In short, do it on a mass-production basis just as the commercial houses do rather than testing your skill on each individual piece.

A chair gets tougher as you stray away from straight cuts. Spindle legs

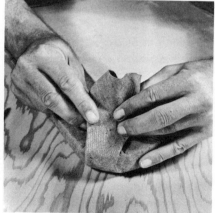

Common method of attaching seat slabs is through the corner block which is used to reinforce the leg-rail assemblies or the seat frames. The screw should not be long enough to pierce the seat.

It is difficult to conceal pleats when the cover material is folded over the seat. The neatest method of folding is shown here. Cut off excess after material is tacked down.

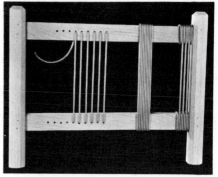

Leather can be used as a seat without a seat-slab or other means of support. Leg-and-rail corner is left exposed. Leather is wrapped around rails and tacked to their inside surfaces.

Three ways to use cord on a straight or curved chair back are shown here. Similar methods can be used on chair seats, but the weave must be closer. Nylon cord, plastic clothesline, rush, reeds and other fibers may all be used.

are harder to attach to rails simply because the mating surfaces are not similar. This is assuming a situation where a straight rail is used to join round legs. Then the end of the rail must be shaped to conform to the contour on the leg. If the round leg slants, or especially if it slants two ways (compound angle), the problem is increased. Here, in addition to conforming to the contours, you must also conform to the angles.

In order to keep things from getting too complex, it's a good idea, when using round legs, to design so the legs will attach directly to a seat frame. If necessary, you can reinforce by using stretchers. Since these will probably be round also, joining them to the legs will involve no more than drilling a hole.

Even dowel joinery can be simplified if you are willing to pay a small price. The chair parts can be assembled under clamps or by using temporary nails. Dowel holes are drilled while the parts are together; then the dowels are glued in place. The price you pay? If you used nails you'll have to hide the holes with wood dough. But whether you worked with nails or with clamps, the system means exposed dowels. They will be less obvious if you make your own from a matching wood and/or by doing a good job and following with patient sanding and good finishing. Or you can make dowels from a contrasting wood and deliberately use them as a decorative detail.

Re-sawing. Often, you can speed up part-making by re-sawing. For example, if you drew the outline of a leg-post on one of the wide surfaces of a piece of 2-by-4 and then cut it out, you could re-saw the cut piece to end up with two duplicates. This holds for legs, or arms, or splats, or backs. If the thickness of the parts you require permits it, you can get more than two duplicates from the single piece of raw stock or, if your equipment permits, you can work with material that is heavier than a 2-by-4.

Finishing Touches. The severity of straight lines can be minimized with pleasing angles and with bevel cuts to remove edges. And it's amazing how you can change the appearance of a piece merely by rounding off all edges with a portable router *after* the parts have been joined.

We used a router on one chair after it had been completely assembled. The stopped router cuts, since we could not work close in to corners where parts joined, merely produced nice detailing. And you are not limited to rounding off edges. Router bits are available in many designs, and can make shaped edges if you desire.

ROUND CHAIRS. The easiest method of making round-chair seats, and one that results in a very strong assembly, consists of a circle formed of segments. You can control grain direction and eliminate weak points. There are situations where you could use a sheet of plywood, of course, but this would involve banding exposed edges and would eliminate, for all practical purposes, rounding off edges. A splined joint is excellent for assembling the segments and is not difficult to do since the spline grooves can be formed after the segments are shaped.

Laminated wooden strips can be used for forming circles or curves. But don't assume that the piece can be bent any old way simply because it's thin. For very sharp turns and tight circles soak the wood, or at least the bend area thoroughly. Best bet is to hold it in boiling water, testing it occasionally, until it's pliable enough to make the turn. Hardwoods such as oak, ash, and walnut bend best.

The kerfing technique is good for circular aprons, especially if you attach blocks to the inside to support the legs and the user's weight. The kerfing technique may also be used when it comes to solid curved backs. Plywood, as well as solid stock, will respond to this treatment. The kerfs can be hidden with sheets of glued-on veneer or similar cover-materials.

By using a system of matching bevel-cuts, you can turn out round shapes from flat boards. If you saw a flat board into wedge-shaped pieces and join the pieces edge to edge, they'll form a complete circle much like wedges from a piece of pie. The only trick to it is that the angles of the saw cuts must add up to 360-degrees.

To figure the cut-angle, divide 360 by the number of pieces you want in the circle. This is the *total* angle that each segment will have. To find the *cut* angle—that is, the angle at which each side of the segment will be cut, divide the *total* angle by two. This is actually the angle at which you set the saw blade. You do have to be accurate, however, when setting the saw blade. Part of a degree doesn't seem like much of an error, but when it is multiplied ten on twenty times it leaves a harrowing gap when you come round to fitting the last segment. Best bet is to check out trial cuts on scrap pieces with a protractor. Make any necessary adjustment before cutting your good stock.

The size of the circle is determined by the number of segments and by the width of the segments. The more segments you use, the closer to a true circle you get, but too many very small pieces can be a problem to assemble. Actually, it will surprise you to discover how little work is required to bring a segmented assembly to full round.

To find the best segment width, make a scaled or full-size layout of a small section of the circle. Then divide the circle into the smallest number of seg-

Wooden frame with a round seat and curved back drilled for weaving. The seat frame slips into notches in the back leg-post. Size the holes according to the diameter of the material you will use to weave. Countersink the holes slightly.

Segments assembled with splines form a strong circular frame. Notice the straight inner edges on the segments. That's because the starting shape was a mitered, square frame. Then the circular shape was cut on the outside edges.

ments that will do the job in line with the thickness of the stock you are using. You'll find that the thinner the stock, the more segments you will require. The segments can be cut to length and then beveled and this is an especially good procedure if you are using up odd lengths of lumber, or you can do the beveling first on long stock and then cut it up into the segment-lengths.

Band clamps would be ideal for holding the segments together during gluing, but strong clothesline twisted tightly about the project will do a satisfactory job. Many times, especially on smaller projects, you can do away with clamping entirely by using staples or corrugated fasteners to hold the parts together until the glue dries. Don't use a lot of glue or the parts will be too slippery to hold in correct alignment. A little film of glue on both edges, allowed to get tacky, is easier to work with and will be equally strong.

A spline joint is very strong and has the advantage of keeping the parts in alignment when you apply clamping pressure. But don't size the splines so they must be forced into the grooves. The splines should fit easily and should leave room for glue. And remember that splines are strongest when they are cut so that the grain runs across the small dimension.

The tongue-and-groove joint also has high strength, but the cuts must be very accurate. Another, quite simple method of assembly is to add one segment after another, gluing and nailing as you go. Work toward two half-circles so you don't close the ring up. The two halfcircles are finally put together under clamps or by stapling. Be careful of nail placement if you use this idea since you don't want to expose them with the sanding (or any turning) that will follow.

TUBULAR CHAIRS. A chair with a tubular frame is often easier to build than one made of wood. The statement will be challenged but only because tubing construction may be a stranger world to most than wood construction. If you bend a length of tubing into a U-shape, you have two legs plus a seat support; no joints, just the two bends. If the bends are opposed, you have a leg, a seat support, and a vertical for the back. Again no joints, just two bends. Two such pieces (with opposed bends) plus one which is U-shaped, tied together with a padded seat and a back, give you a complete chair.

You can use tubing such as do-it-yourself aluminum together with all the fittings that are available for forming tubing joints, or you can use electrical conduit, perhaps painted flat-black to resemble wrought iron. If you are familiar with metal-working and own welding equipment, you have no problem. Otherwise you can do all the bending and have the welding done for you at a local metal-working shop. Or you can use mechanical fasteners. Nuts and bolts, sheet-metal screws, even wood screws can be used and, most times, can be hidden effectively.

Most bends can be fairly generous; this makes the job easier. The best bet is to use oversize lengths and trim to size after the bends are made. For conduit, you can use an ordinary tube bender. You can buy one for about eight dollars, or you can rent one.

Don't worry if the tube flattens a little in the bend area. To minimize this, use the old dodge of packing the tube with damp sand before you make the bend. Tamp the sand firmly in place with a dowel. This will support tubing walls and keep them from crimping in the bend area. To get uniform bends you can shape curved blocks around which to make bends or to use as checks if you bend with other equipment.

One trick that will let you skip bending procedures completely is to use

Tubular chairs are not difficult to construct as long as you stick to simple lines—at least to begin with. For example, only three pieces of tubing were used to make these chairs. The lounge chair at the right is a continuous loop with the ends joined by welding, with a sleeve, or with an internal wooden dowel.

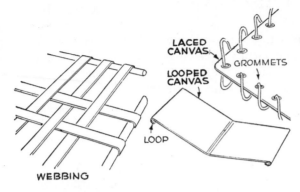

LACED CANVAS

GROMMETS

LOOPED CANVAS

LOOP

WEBBING

Here are three ways to install seats and backs on tubular frames. Plastic bands, folded and grommeted at the ends, can be attached to the tubing with sheet-metal screws and woven across the opening. Canvas can be looped over the top and front frame or laced through holes in the tubing. Other ideas: wooden slats screwed through holes in the tubing; plastic rope wrapped around frame.

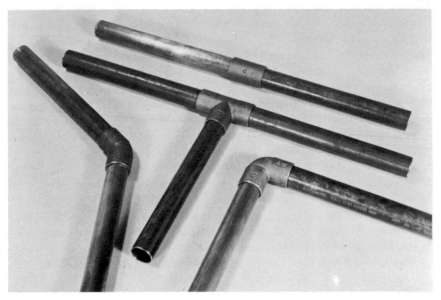

These are examples of commercial fittings you can buy to assemble copper tubing. Note the various turns you can make without having to bend the tubing. Fittings like these are sweat-soldered. The tubing and the fittings can be polished and lacquered, or they can be painted flat black to resemble wrought iron.

commercial fittings, sold as accessories for copper pipe, electrical conduit and do-it-yourself aluminum. This greatly simplifies construction, and lets you work with straight lengths of tubing which you can easily cut to the exact length required. This is a great help since most of the homecraftsman's problems with tube bending arise from trying to make the same bend in exactly the right place on similar pieces of tubing.

On do-it-yourself aluminum, fittings are mechanical; you just drill holes and tighten screws. This is something you can remember for knock-down projects. Fittings for copper tubing and pipe are sweat-soldered, which is simple to do if you own a small propane torch.

There are two special items you should have to work more efficiently with tubing—one is a V-block, the other is a tube-cutter. The V-block lets you position tubing accurately under a spindle for drilling radial holes. The tube-cutter slices tubes cleanly and is far superior to using a saw and a file. Tube-cutters are not expensive, and if you plan any project at all that involves tubing it's wise to get one.

Metal tubing can also be combined with wood. Special flanges are available for attaching pipe legs to woden frames. If you want to slant the leg, use a wooden wedge between the flange and the seat or frame.

Non-threaded tubing such as aluminum or copper designed for assembly with ready-made fittings can be attached, for example, by plugging the tube tightly with a dowel and using the lock-wedge technique either hidden or exposed.

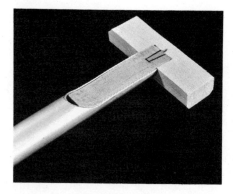

Wood plugs can be used to join tubing to wood. The dowel plug must be tight in the tube; it wouldn't hurt to add a lock-dowel also. Lock-wedge (and the plug) can be through, or hidden as shown above in cut-away cross section.

Feet for tubing legs are available in many forms. Everything you see here can be bought at hardware counters. Most of the tips are resilient to protect floors. Steel glides (at right) are held by wood plugs driven into the tube.

CHAPTER TWENTY-TWO

BED FRAMES

THE PURPOSE of a bed frame is to elevate a mattress above the floor. As such it doesn't have to be more than a leg-rail assembly with some special provision on which the mattress, or spring, can rest. Rear legs-and-rail, and the front legs-and-rail are separate assemblies connected by the longer, side rails. The connection joint between side rails and end assemblies is demountable; thus the bed can be knocked-down for moving. Many designs do not extend beyond the basic leg-and-rail so that when the bed is made up, the frame is hardly visible. Ready-made metal frames are available (and used very generally today), and these can be mounted on wooden or steel legs, with or without casters. These may be used as they are without any elaboration, or they can be the basis around which you can design, for example, a storage headboard.

Overall mattress dimensions vary. A "queen's bed" mattress is about 6′ 4″ by 7′ 2″; a "king-size" mattress would be even larger. A mattress for a regular-

Bed frame is a simple construction of separate end assemblies joined by rails . . .

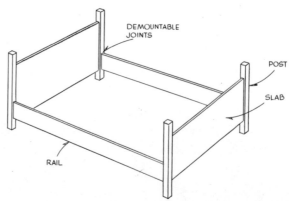

Ends may be posts and bars . . . a framed slab . . . or posts and shaped slab . . .

But you can experiment with your own designs . . .

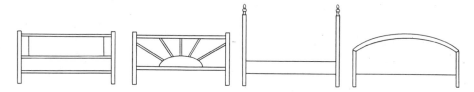

Ends may be the same height . . . head may be taller than the foot . . . or the foot may be a continuation of the rails . . .

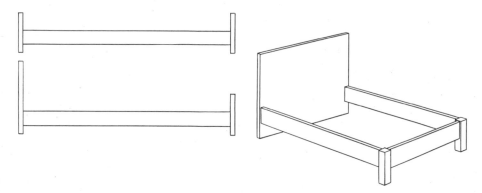

size single bed would be about 3′ 2″ by 6′ 2″. And there are sizes between— twin bed, small three-quarter bed, large three-quarter bed, double bed. These are the mattress dimensions and represent the inside dimensions of the frame; that is, from inside surface of rail to the inside surface of the opposite rail. Over-all dimensions would be greater. Bed height—the distance from the floor to the top of the mattress—is about 20″.

Best bet when making a frame is to have the springs and mattresses on hand or, at least, after deciding on what size bed you want, to visit a store and measure the units. Thus you can design around what are the most critical dimensions.

Don't make any attempt to concoct your own variety of demountable joint. The available hardware is too good and the cost is minimal. Fixed joints at

To make rail-to-post joint demountable, use special hardware . . .

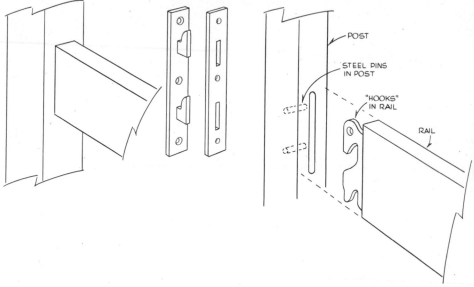

POST

STEEL PINS
IN POST

"HOOKS"
IN RAIL

RAIL

Slats for box spring rest on cleats attached firmly to the rails . . .

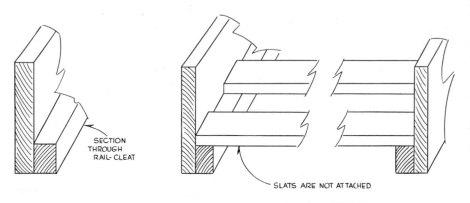

SECTION
THROUGH
RAIL-CLEAT

SLATS ARE NOT ATTACHED

those points may be considered (although not recommended) only if the frame is of the very basic variety—that is, a platform to elevate the mattress. Ready-made steel frames are made so but they are easily transported without having to be dismantled.

The bed frame can be simple or elaborate. It can be a steel frame pushed against the wall with a decorative headboard attached to the wall itself. It can involve a storage-type headboard or one which can serve functionally as bookshelves, radio shelf, side tables, etc.

In any event, the basic consideration as far as construction is concerned is to picture the project as being two end assemblies which are connected by the side rails. When you decide on a furniture-type headboard, design it as if you were going to use it as a free-standing unit. The foot-end is seldom designed for any function beyond supporting the springs and mattresses.

Headboard can be designed as a storage unit . . .

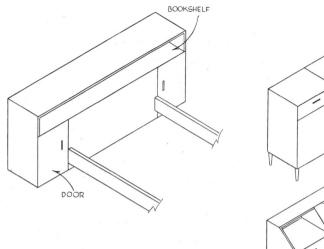

BOOKSHELF

DOOR

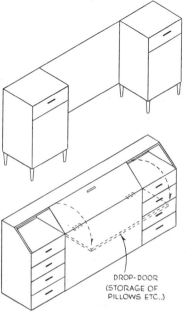

DROP-DOOR
(STORAGE OF
PILLOWS ETC..)

GLOSSARY

APRON   A strip of wood at the base of cabinets, table tops and chair seats, sometimes called a RAIL.

ARM SUPPORT   A curved or vertical piece supporting the front end of a chair arm.

BALL FOOT   A ball-like, often ornamental end of a furniture leg.

BANDING   Strips of wood or VENEER used to conceal the edge grain of plywood or other stock. Also, a strip of contrasting wood inlaid in a surface.

BEVEL   The sloping edge of a board which forms an angle greater or less than 90 degrees with the surface.

BOARD FOOT   A unit of measurement by which board lumber is priced, represented by a piece 1″ by 1′ by 1′ or its cubic equivalent.

BUFFET   A small cupboard or sideboard for keeping dishes and silverware.

BUREAU   A chest of drawers, usually for the bedroom. In England and France, a writing desk with drawers.

BUTT HINGE   A hinge fastened to the edge of a door and the side of a case, usually mortised into both.

BUTT JOINT   A joint made by abutting one member against another, edge to edge or edge to surface, and held by glue and/or nails or screws.

CABRIOLE LEG   A furniture leg in many variations that swells outward at the upper part and inward at the lower part.

CASE (CASE GOODS)   A general term in furniture building that designates any box-like piece with doors, drawers or shelves, such as cabinets, chests, bookcases, etc.

CASTERS   Wheels or cased ball bearings placed in the base of a project to provide mobility.

CHAMFER   In essence, a BEVEL which does not remove the entire edge of the stock.

CHANNEL   A shape which is like a DADO or GROOVE.

CORNER BLOCK   A wooden block which reinforces the corners of a frame assembly.

COUNTERBORE   To recess the head of a screw or other fastener below the surface of the wood in order to conceal it with a dowel plug.

COUNTERSINK   To drill a conical depression at the mouth of a screw hole to set a flathead screw flush with or below the surface. Also, the tool employed to accomplish this purpose.

COVE   A concave shape; moulding with all or part of its face having a concave cross section.

DADO   A U-shaped cut made across the grain of a board.

DADO HEAD   A special tool for a radial-arm or table saw for cutting dadoes, grooves, rabbets, etc.

DADO JOINT   Joining two boards by fitting the edge of one into a DADO cut in the surface of the other.

DENTIL   A classic design which is actually a series of equally spaced rectangular blocks.

DIVIDER   A partition in a cabinet or drawer.

DOVETAIL   A joint made by cutting a series of projections in the ends of two boards so they interlock at right angles.

DOWEL   A wooden stick ⅛" to 1½" in diameter and about 3' long, used for making furniture joints, plugging screw holes and other purposes.

DOWEL JOINT   In its simplest form, a butt joint reinforced with dowels glued in holes in both members.

DOWEL PINS   Short pieces of dowel with chamfered ends and spiraled so glue will spread. Can be purchased "ready-made."

DROP DOOR   A door that is hinged at the bottom and opens outward, sometimes supported at the horizontal position by a bracket so it can be used as a writing or serving surface.

DROP LEAF   A hinged table leaf that folds down when not in use.

DUST PANEL   A horizontal partition, usually of hardboard or thin plywood, between drawers in a chest.

EARLY AMERICAN   Furniture style of the Colonial and post-Revolutionary periods in America (1620-1847).

EDGE-GLUE   To glue two or more boards edge-to-edge to make a broad panel.

ESCUTCHEON PINS   Small, sharply-pointed nails with half-round heads, often obtained in copper or brass and used decoratively.

ESCUTCHEON PLATE   A shield-shaped, decorative metal fitting for a keyhole.

FACE FRAME   A frame of narrow stock applied to the front of a case to conceal joints and edge grain and to provide a broad surface for hanging doors.

FILLER   A liquid or paste used to fill the grain of wood and to produce a smooth surface for finishing.

FINIAL   The piece, usually decorative, used at the end of uprights.

GLUE BLOCK   A block of wood glued at the inside corner of a furniture joint to reinforce it.

GROOVE   A U-shaped cut made *with* the grain of the wood.

GUIDE BAR   In a chest of drawers, a wooden bar on which a runner attached to the drawer bottom can slide.

HARDBOARD   A grainless, durable panel made of wood chips which have been pressed at high temperature.

HARDWOOD   Wood of deciduous trees such as oak, ash, walnut, maple.

HIGHBOY　A tall chest of drawers.

HUTCH　A cupboard with doors surmounted by a set of shelves.

JIG　A device, often homemade, to guide a tool or anchor the work in the correct position in relation with the tool.

JOINT　The point at which two pieces of wood are fitted together to form a permanent bond.

KERF　The cut made by a saw blade.

KERFING　Sawing a series of cuts in a piece of wood so it can be bent or rounded.

KIDNEY　Description of the shape of a desk, table, etc., in which the top has the shape of a kidney bean.

LAP JOINT　Uniting two pieces of wood by overlapping their surfaces, usually by cutting away half the thickness of each piece so their surfaces are flush.

LATH　A strip of wood, usually 1½″ by ⅜″ by 4′ long.

LEG-AND-RAIL ASSEMBLY　A method of attaching legs to a piece of furniture. The legs are braced by the rails, which are then attached to the furniture's undersurface.

LOCK-DOWEL　A dowel which strengthens a joint and prevents separation even when the glue fails.

LOUVER　One of a series of angled slats in a door or shutter which permit ventilation but exclude vision.

MITER JOINT　A joint between two members in which each is cut at an angle.

MORTISE　A hole or cavity cut in one member to receive all or part of another.

MORTISE-AND-TENON JOINT　A furniture joint accomplished by fitting a TENON on one member into a MORTISE in the other.

MOULDING　Strips of wood formed into various contours, used for decorative purposes.

PARTICLEBOARD　A hard, durable panel of pressed wood chips or other materials which has many structural uses.

PEDESTAL　Usually a base component; a tall, narrow support for a decorative item such as a statue or a plant.

PILOT HOLE　The hole that is drilled to receive the threaded part of a screw.

PLUG CUTTER　Tool used to form short pieces of dowel which may be used to plug counterbored screw holes, or in joints.

POST　The corner piece on any furniture; the corner post of a bed.

RABBET　An L-shaped cut in the edge of a board.

RABBET JOINT　Joining two boards by fitting the edge of one into a rabbet cut in the other.

RAIL　A horizontal bar of wood that joins two other pieces, also called an APRON in certain cases.

REEDING　Raised parallel lines of convex or beaded form on the surface of wood, usually on moulding. The reverse of *fluting*.

ROUTER   A power-driven woodworking tool for cutting depressions and shaping edges.

RUNNER   A concave bar of wood attached to the bottom of a drawer and which fits the GUIDE BAR.

SCALLOP   A series of semicircular or recessed curves in the edge of a board.

SCROLL   Often used to mean the same as SPIRAL; actually an ornamental spiral line.

SEALER   A liquid compound applied to wood which equalizes the hard and soft grains and makes possible an evenly toned finish.

SERRATED   Shaped basically like the teeth on a saw.

SET   To drive a nail head beneath the surface of the wood so it can be concealed with putty or plastic wood.

SHANK HOLE   In joining two boards with screws, the hole that is drilled to receive the upper, non-threaded part of the screw.

SKIRT   Similar to APRON.

SOFTWOOD   Wood from conifers (evergreens) such as pine, fir and spruce.

SPIRAL   A twisting form; same effect obtained by twisting together several strands of wire or string.

SPLAT   A centerpiece in a chair back.

SPLINE   A thin piece of wood inserted in grooves cut in the mating edges of a joint in order to strengthen the joint.

STILE   A vertical member of a door frame against which the door is fitted.

STRETCHER   A horizontal bar connecting, and thus bracing, two legs.

TENON   A tongue or projection shaped to fit into a MORTISE.

TAMBOUR DOOR   A door composed of strips of wood glued to a flexible backing so that it can slide in curved grooves.

TONGUE-AND-GROOVE   Milled lumber having a groove in one edge and a matching tongue on the other.

VENEER   Thin sheet of fine wood used to cover inferior stock to produce a decorative finish.

WARPED   Term applied when a board is twisted out of shape due to temperature and moisture conditions.

INDEX